Being in Common

The Bucknell Studies in Latin American Literature and Theory
Series Editor: Aníbal González, Pennsylvania State University

The literature of Latin America, with its intensely critical, self-questioning, and experimental impulses, is currently one of the most influential in the world. In its earlier phases, this literary tradition produced major writers, such as Bartolomé de las Casas, Bernal Díaz del Castillo, the Inca Garcilaso, Sor Juana Inés de la Cruz, Andrés Bello, Gertrudis Gómez de Avellaneda, Domingo F. Sarmiento, José Martí, and Rubén Darío. More recently, writers from the U.S. to China, from Britain to Africa and India, and of course from the Iberian Peninsula, have felt the impact of the fiction and the poetry of such contemporary Latin American writers as Borges, Cortázar, Garcia Márquez, Guimarães Rosa, Lezama Lima, Neruda, Vargas Llosa, Paz, Poniatowska, and Lispector, among many others. Dealing with far-reaching questions of history and modernity, language and selfhood, and power and ethics, Latin American literature sheds light on the many-faceted nature of Latin American life, as well as on the human condition as a whole.

The aim of this series of books is to provide a forum for the best criticism on Latin American literature in a wide range of critical approaches, with an emphasis on works that productively combine scholarship with theory. Acknowledging the historical links and cultural affinities between Latin American and Iberian literatures, the series welcomes consideration of Spanish and Portuguese texts and topics, while also providing a space of convergence for scholars working in Romance studies, comparative literature, cultural studies, and literary theory.

Titles in Series

Being in Common

Nation, Subject, and Community in Latin American Literature and Culture

Silvia N. Rosman

Lewisburg
Bucknell University Press
London: Associated University Presses

Associated University Presses
2010 Eastpark Boulevard
Cranbury, NJ 08512

Associated University Presses
Unit 304, the Chandlery
50 Westminster Bridge Road
London SE1 7QY, England

Associated University Presses
P.O. Box 338, Port Credit
Mississauga, Ontario
Canada L5G 4L8

The paper used in this publication meets the requirements of the American National Standard for Permanence of Paper for Printed Library Materials Z39.48-1984.

Library of Congress Cataloging-in-Publication Data

Rosman, Silvia Nora, 1959–
    Being in common : nation, subject, and community in Latin American literature and culture / Silvia N. Rosman.
        p.   cm.—(Bucknell studies in Latin American literature and theory)
    Includes bibliographical references and index.
    ISBN 0-8387-5552-6 (alk. paper)
    1. Spanish American literature—20th century—History and criticism. 2. National characteristics, Latin American, in literature.   3. Carpentier, Alejo, 1904–   Pasos perdidos.   4. Martâinez Estrada, Ezequiel, 1895–1964.   5. Paz, Octavio, 1914–   6. Borges, Jorge Luis, 1899–   I. Title.   II. Series.
PQ7081.R672   2003
860.9′98′0904—dc21   2002153093

PRINTED IN THE UNITED STATES OF AMERICA

Contents

Acknowledgments

THERE ARE MANY PEOPLE WHO, THROUGHOUT THE YEARS, HAVE made *Being in Common* possible. I would first like to thank Sylvia Molloy—mentor, colleague, and valued interlocutor—for her warm support as well as for her comments and suggestions on various chapters of this book. Kathleen Ross has been a constant source of advice, support and good cheer. Thanks also go to Eduardo Subirats and Marta Peixoto.

Parts of this book were presented at conferences, colloquia, and graduate seminars in the Department of Spanish and Portuguese, the King Juan Carlos I of Spain Center, the Center for Latin American and Caribbean Studies, and the Scholar's Program, all at New York University. I thank the organizers, as well as friends, colleagues and students for their comments and suggestions. Warm thanks also go to Luis Fernández-Cifuentes for giving me the opportunity to present my work at Harvard University, as well as for his constant friendship, support and interest in my work. I am grateful for an invitation from Adriana Astutti to speak at the Facultad de Humanidades y Artes, Universidad Nacional de Rosario, Argentina and wish to acknowledge the suggestions and comments of Carlos Alonso.

Research support was made possible by a New York University Research Challenge Fund and the Center for Latin American and Caribbean Studies at New York University.

An earlier version of part of Chapter 2 was published in *Latin American Literary Review* 26, no. 51 (1998). I acknowledge permission to reprint.

My editor Aníbal González Perez was enthusiastic about this project from the start; his help and encouragement are greatly appreciated.

Being in Common is dedicated to Gabriel Riera.

Being in Common

Introduction: The Interrupted Quest: Rethinking Nation, Subject, and Community in Latin American Literature and Culture

PREFACE

WHAT IS THE FORCE OF THE IDEA OF COMMUNITY, WHAT PARTICULAR appeal does it hold despite evidence of its dislocation or dissolution, despite the sexism, xenophobia, racism, and war which should be a testament to community's non-existence? While contemporary criticism questions the notion of an immanent unity or totality, the relation to others and the meanings of being in common remain central problematics in discussions of ethics, writing, and politics. Now more than ever a dismantling or demystification of the essentialist concepts that sustained traditional notions of community (Nation, State, People, Identity, Language, Literature) is known to be insufficient, prey as these concepts are to re-inscription as foundational categories.

Postcolonial criticism and, more recently, postnational, transnational, and globalization theories, as we will discuss in detail below, all attempt to articulate forms of the collective that presuppose the breakdown of the nation state as the guarantor of communal identification. If the nation is no longer the imagined community, to borrow Benedict Anderson's well-known expression, these approaches propose, in different ways, that the formation of a "we" is still possible on the borders and interstices of what earlier could be called the nation. Where traditionally the nation space defines itself through a series of (often violent) exclusions, those very peoples (migrants, immigrants, minorities) that the nation leaves out of its imaginary unity accomplish its dis-location. The counter-narratives of these peoples thus challenge the homogeneity of traditional national narratives. However, these theories of the "post" are still tied to the nation, even as they affirm its collapse as a defining and delimiting concept. Postcolonial and postnational narratives must necessarily represent (identify and localize) where and by whom the dislocation of the nation takes place.

Contemporary studies of Latin American literature and culture have also moved away from the totalizing concept of nation, but still maintain the quest of identity as a frame for articulating how literary and cultural texts express and produce forms of the collective. Whether the quest is the hermeneutic construct for reading Latin American texts since the nineteenth century or a paradigm that must be superseded in a postmodern or globalized context, the quest of identity remains an enduring structural element in critical analysis.

As in postcolonial and postnational narratives, Latin American literary and cultural criticism also relies on substantive representations of places and identities in order to articulate forms of collective experience. Contemporary critical discourse is thus caught in a paradoxical position: it is no longer able to sustain holistic and homogenous narratives of identity and identification, but must nevertheless presuppose the particularity and uniqueness of its object of study: namely, Latin American literature and culture. The problem is seemingly unavoidable: how does one study the singularity of a literary or cultural text without grounding it in some form, without assigning it a place? How do criticism and theory avoid in their own discourses the quest of identity that supposedly they are attempting to decompose? Symptomatic of this problem is the question that Carlos Alonso formulates in his *Spanish American Regional Novel*: "will there ever be a Latin American discourse that is no longer centered on either the question of identity or its dismantling?"[1] Although Alonso clearly wishes to articulate an alternative reading of Latin American literary and cultural texts, he acknowledges, as do most recent critical studies, that "the topic of cultural essence will [not] lose its sway."[2]

Being in Common studies the implications of the present critical impasse by exploring some of the key paradigms that articulate the study of Latin American literature and culture. One such paradigm, as we mentioned, is the quest of identity. My analysis shows that allegories of the quest of identity are not the ultimate destiny of Latin American texts, nor a necessarily authorizing critical paradigm. Neither simply undermining foundational or essentializing categories nor replacing them with the negative equivalent of those same categories (and thus risk repeating the quest paradigm), *Being in Common* analyzes how literary and cultural texts interrupt the quest of identity in order to show its limits. These texts destabilize the concepts that have been the staple of Latin American literary and critical production since the nineteenth century. The liminality they expose, therefore, gestures toward articulations of community that do not depend on direct representations and pre-defined identities.

QUEST NARRATIVES

Experimentando los primeros síntomas de la oscura irrealidad general que se avecinaba, buscaban empecinados una respuesta, sin comprender que, insospechadamente, la respuesta estaba en la necesidad que habían tenido de formularse la pregunta.

[Experiencing the first symptoms of the dark general unreality that was approaching, they stubbornly sought an answer, without understanding that, unknown to them, the answer was in the need of having had to pose the question.]
—Juan José Saer, *El río sin orillas*

The question of national identity has often been framed as a quest narrative in Latin American texts, as well as in Latin American literary and cultural criticism. Since the nineteenth century, post-independence Latin America has sought, according to many critics, to posit an identity capable of both defining its difference in relation to the metropolitan centers and of containing those internal forces (mestizo and indigenous groups) which might put in doubt the unity of the *independentista* projects.[3] Thus, in Martin S. Stabb's study of the essay genre, Latin America is characterized as being in a constant quest of identity. For Stabb, writers as diverse as Domingo Faustino Sarmiento, Alfonso Reyes and Pedro Henríquez Ureña continuously search for a key which will provide the answer, unravel the mystery, provide a cure, and allow for the desired representation of the nation space as an organic and homogenous whole and the "People as One." In the conclusion to his study Stabb affirms the "yearning for communion with all men" that is an intrinsic part of Latin American texts.[4]

Yet true to the concept of quest which presents human experience as an aporia (literally, absence of a road), identity constructions have also been shown to resist (but not necessarily defy) the teleological paradigm outlined above. For Djelal Kadir, Latin American

texts' quest of identity are, in fact, questing fictions, where the
search is a spectral undertaking: instead of closure, unity, identity,
there is errancy, divagation. The home, as absolute origin and end
of meaning, the "place" of identity itself, is forever displaced: "the
poetic quest in the texts we now read carries on as unremitting peri-
petia. Products of an antipodal 'other world,' these texts obses-
sively move to engender and flaunt their own 'otherness,' their own
non-identity to themselves."[5] For Kadir, Latin American quest ro-
mances ceaselessly repeat (each time differently) Columbus's errant inaugural scene of discovery and by so doing "pursue the
attainment of novelty by constantly aiming at displacement so that
[they] may move to the originary point of departure, to the beginning."[6] Kadir thus places a limit on the errant Latin American quest
in order to affirm its self-engendering history and to displace its
status as the unfulfilled Other of European desire. The critical discourse and the texts studied participate in a specular relation, both
affirming the quest's reason for being, as well as an authentic and
autonomous identity always already known to exist.

More than just a motif in critical analyses of Latin American literature and culture, the quest and the question of identity are inex-
tricably linked. In order to understand why, we will now focus on
the relation between quest or travel and the movement of critical
thought, a traditional topos in literature and philosophy. The epigraph from Juan José Saer, for example, speaks of the first explorers to the River Plate region and in so doing provides a model for
the critical act itself: the "meaning" which the explorers quest for
is the quest itself. The seemingly tautological movement of this
statement can be better understood by making a detour into the theory of travel.

In his study of travel narratives, Georges Van Den Abbeele points
to the connection between the figure of travel and the elaboration of
a critical discourse. He shows that this figure depends on an economy at the center of which stands the home (*oikos*) as a referential
point of origin or end. Whether travel is seen in terms of gain (progress, self-awareness, knowledge) or loss (expropriation, exile,
death: the ultimate journey), the home functions as the absolute beginning and end of all meaning—identity itself. Paradoxically,
travel serves as an expansive and also limiting figure because if origin and destination remain the same, no travel can occur. A tension
is established, then, between an economic concept of travel that
seeks to domesticate, to make familiar, and travel as transgressive

and disruptive, where borders are crossed and divagation or wandering may occur. The home, as the locus that imposes the limits on travel, constantly runs the risk of being displaced.[7]

What are the implications for the critical text itself if Latin American works are so often read as quest narratives? Does the critical text repeat the quest and follow its same itinerary? Inasmuch as the quest is seen as a space of writing, it presupposes a topography, the writing of a demarcated space, which in the case of Latin American critical texts we have mentioned, implies writing the space of Latin American identity. In fact, the two modalities of the quest narrative discussed thus far (the quest for self-identity and communion and the quest as displacement and errancy), both point to the dual locus of critical discourse as outlined in the economy of travel above. These quest narratives depend on the notion of the *oikos* (home) as self-referential point of origin or departure—even if that *oikos*, as in the case of Kadir, proves to be the fiction of a fiction.

The inextricable relation between the quests of identity in Latin American texts and in critical discourse becomes evident when one considers the problem of temporality. The quests for identity point to both the unfinished project that is Latin America but also to the uniqueness that is its essence. That is, they propose an expansive, un-ending, even wandering path for seeking identity while at the same time delimiting and thus prescribing the distance those quests can cover. One could say that even the most traditional of quest narratives already allow for a permanent un-homeliness while simultaneously anchoring the discourse in an ahistorical, transcendent essence.

This impasse can be glimpsed in the strange temporality of the nation's telling. In the quests of identity what must be found (the answer, the meaning) must also be the nation's foundation. A temporal displacement thus becomes the hallmark of these searches. The elusive also becomes the bedrock, the moment to come and the immemorial past are joined together and become one—teleological, eschatological. The end must be the beginning and the object looked for thus becomes an immutable essence.[8]

The aporias at work in the quest of identity are constitutive of the very concept of nation, as Slavoj Žižek has noted:

On the one hand, "nation" of course designates modern community delivered of the traditional "organic" ties, a community in which the premodern links tying down the individual to a particular estate, family, religious group, and so on, are broken—the traditional corporate community is replaced by the modern nation-state whose constituents are "citizens": people as abstract individuals, not as members of particular estates, and so forth. On the other hand, "nation" can never be reduced to a network of purely symbolic ties: there is always a kind of "surplus of the Real" that sticks to it—to define itself, "national identity" must appeal to the contingent materiality of the "common roots", of "blood and soil", and so on. In short, "nation" designates at one and the same time the instance by means of reference to which traditional "organic" links are dissolved *and* the "remainder of the pre-modern in modernity."[9]

Žižek finds that the concept of nation depends on the rhetoric of modernity as well as on traditional paradigms of community. This ambiguous temporality, which is proper to modernity's conceptual apparatus, shows that simply destabilizing, de-centering, or re-semanticizing those concepts is insufficient, given that all such strategies are already inscribed in the concepts themselves. Modernity is the name of that aporetic relation in which all definitions of the "new" are inevitably tied and, in fact, depend on what they define themselves against.[10] Given the inherent contradictions in the concepts that make up our critical vocabulary, it appears that literary and cultural criticism must unpack the conceptual frameworks of texts in order not to localize and fix their meaning (even if that meaning is found to be ambiguity or paradox), but to mark the limit of all such localizations. In other words, to read texts in order to not only undermine or question the grounds on which they rely, but to question and therefore write presupposing the removal of those grounds.

If quest narratives, the staple of Latin American literary, cultural, and critical production since the nineteenth century,[11] must always posit a reference point through which to read the voyage undertaken and, in that way, anchor it, define it, and understand it in some way, then we must be cognizant of the fact that the question of travel and the positing of a theory cannot be thought separately, even though they seem to be at cross-purposes. But if undermining the theory is also presupposed in the quest, then it becomes imperative to think both the travel and the theory differently.

Roberto González Echevarría's *Voice of the Masters* makes clear the need for contemporary criticism to think beyond traditional notions regarding the uniqueness and unity of Latin American literature and culture and to find a way out of the quest of identity:

In the functioning of literature as an institution the concept of culture is a key element. Remove the concept of culture and its corollary of national identity from the language of Latin American literature and that literature becomes nearly silent. Yet Latin American literature, instead of contributing to the elaboration of a concept of culture, takes shape as it attempts to dismantle that concept in a contrary, negative structure that becomes its most salient and positive characteristic . . . However, the purpose of such an examination should not be to do away with the concept of culture and the idea of literature, but rather to interpret the sense and the inner workings of the relationship between the two . . . It is not that a mystification must be denounced, but rather that its mechanisms must be dismantled, since such a dismantling will reveal not information but the critical substratum of Latin American literature of which Paz speaks. In this substratum, in which apparent doctrine becomes polemical confrontation, the different components of the text bristle and pulsate instead of bending before the soothing breeze of doctrine.[12]

González Echevarría acknowledges the ideological basis of concepts such as literature and culture and, therefore, calls for their dismantling. Yet one can also observe that a dismantling of the concepts cannot only be ideological because the critical discourse that Latin American texts elicit reinserts a substratum (an underlying support or foundation) through which those very dismantled concepts will once again be viable ones for the critic. In other words, in González Echevarría's proposal the impossibility of utilizing essentializing categories in order to read Latin American texts goes hand in hand with the parallel gesture of interpreting the sense of the relation between culture and literature. The double meaning of the word sense (as meaning and as direction) thus threatens to re-inscribe the economy of travel we outlined above, given that sense can again become a dwelling place, a permanent place or foundation for what would be delimited, defined, and represented as Latin American culture and literature.

If the relation between travel and theory is such that one cannot talk about one without drifting into the other, then why travel if the destination is already known or at least surmised; can one travel without knowing when the traveling will stop? What would be entailed in such an enterprise and would we still be able to call it a critical one? In other words, what are the possibilities and impossibilities of the category "Latin American criticism" if the pre-determined grids by which we approach our objects of study are no longer valid?

Theories of Nation and Community

Despite the permanent tension between movement and stasis that marks the concept of nation, traditional national narratives have foregrounded the homogeneity and unity of their localizing function. Even as the internal wars of nineteenth-century Argentina testified to the fragmentation of the newly formed nation, D. F. Sarmiento vehemently proclaimed, "La República Argentina es una e indivisible" [The Argentine Republic is one and indivisible].[13] Postcolonial criticism has convincingly shown that national narratives, produced through various mediums as forms of political containment, as well as to insure the acquisition and retention of state power, must continuously reproduce the historical and future existence of the People as One. Indeed, it is the unity of the multiple that these narratives offer, specular narratives where the many (despite real and violent exclusions) recognize themselves as a National Subject. I will discuss below how postcolonial criticism, as well as theories of globalization and the postnational, make problematic this traditional schema of national narratives, as well as how these theories relate to our analysis of Latin American literary and cultural texts.

Benedict Anderson's imagined community of the nation depends on a certain definition of the concept of "subject", which is necessary in order to elucidate any question of identity formation and, therefore, of community.[14] Recent studies on community have shown that the West derives its notions of the communal starting from the self-generating, originary Cartesian subject whose independence from all objecthood makes any appeal to alterity difficult, if not impossible.[15] The very etymology of the word community is indicative of the problem. Whether considered as *com-munis* (in the sense of mutual obligation or indebtedness, as in the social contract) or *com-unus* (together as one), the immanent Cartesian subject is at the center of the definition of community.

In both these definitions, the individual subsumes all notions of collectivity, whether the community is considered in terms of a total fusion (as in communion, the "People as One") where all differences are obviated or as in the social contract, that presumes the prior constitution of self-determining subjects who then come together to form a community. As Van Den Abbeele attests, "both organicist and contractual theories of community conceal the essentialism of a subject immanent to itself, which speaks either for and as a whole that would precede the parts (*com-unus*) or as a part that is itself already a whole before its encounter with other 'parts' (*com-munis*)."[16] *Webster's Dictionary* sums up the problem well: "we" is defined as "I" plus the rest of the group.

Anderson's imagined community of the nation exemplifies this notion of immanence and the temporality that is its effect. The imaginary characteristic of nation formation allows for the anonymous subject of communal fusion embedded in the homogeneous empty time of historical continuity. Although Anderson does situate the late nineteenth-century Americas of the post-independence period as living the Benjaminian *jetzseit* of a revolutionary now time, which breaks that continuum, it is short lived, and homogenous empty time quickly becomes the time of the nation's imagining.

As some critics have observed, Anderson's schema misses the iterative component of national discourse and as such is unable to read historical difference.[17] Perhaps more importantly, the homogenous temporality of the imagined community does not allow for the possibility of imagining differences within that same community. Indeed, San Martín's 1821 decree declaring the indigenous and creole populations equally worthy of the name Peruvian must necessarily speak of another notion of community than what could be imagined by either of those groups. This makes clear that the imagined community is not just "an abstract idea" but, rather, a normative and often violent means of achieving homogeneity. Anderson's schema thus leads to the imagined community as essence, as a timeless ground subsuming the concept of nation.

The totalizing characteristic of historicist narratives was already made problematic by Walter Benjamin in his "Theses on the Philosophy of History," where he proposes that the fragmentary images of *jetzseit* (now time) interrupt history conceived as a continuum. These images which "flit by" and are always in a state of disappearing are fragments that follow but do not match one another. Thus, no identity, no repetition of the same, can be found there. They are like "broken parts of a vessel" from which no totality can be reconstituted.

The postcolonial critic Homi Bhabha takes up Benjamin's notion of *jetzseit* in his study of national narratives, which in part means to complicate Anderson's schema. Bhabha distinguishes between pedagogical and performative narratives in order to demonstrate

that the performative narrative of the minority or the oppressed interrupts the temporality of pedagogical (i.e. historicist) national
narratives:

> The pedagogical founds its narrative authority in a tradition of the peo-
> ple . . . encapsulated in a succession of historical moments that repre-
> sents an eternity produced by self-generation. The performative
> intervenes in the sovereignty of the nation's self-generation by casting
> a shadow between the people as 'image' and its signification as a differ-
> entiating sign of Self, distinct from the Other or the Outside.[18]

Bhabha's performative narrative intends to reinstate a historical
dimension into an otherwise homogenizing time-line, as well as to
show that the exclusions that form the basis of historicist narratives
interrupt and destabilize those narratives and, therefore, put in
doubt the fiction of the People as One. Because Bhabha clearly does
not wish to equate historicist and resistant narratives, the performative temporality that interrupts the pedagogical is only supposed to
cast a "shadow" and not become a representation itself, lest it risk
becoming the underside of the oppressive exclusionary force. However, later on in the essay this "shadow" manifests itself as the
babelic voices of the minority and the oppressed: as counter-repre-
sentations.
   Although Bhabha's performative narrative is clearly modeled on
Benjamin's "now time," for the latter historicist narrative discourse
can be interrupted precisely because "now time" cannot be represented. In Benjamin's notion of *jetzseit* there is a constricting of
"the instantaneous particular, and always perishing *jetzt* and the
chronological general, and durative *zeit*—gathering them by way of
an abbreviation which instantiates the very notion of now time."[19]
In Bhabha's schema these become the performative and the pedagogical, respectively. Unlike Bhabha, however, Benjamin's *jetzseit*
"implies a past filled with images which are neither merely present
in, nor simply represented by, history. Rather, the now time saturat-
ing the past presents the present with an image in which it may recognize itself. It makes the present come or emerge . . . Neither
exactly disjunction, not precisely connective *jetzseit* cannot be
thought of *substantially*, however much in the negative."[20] Benjamin's interruptive "now time" creates images that are not representations and therefore cannot become identifiable objects of
discourse.

Benjamin's notion of historical fragmentariness makes problematic Anderson's contention that nations "engender the need for a narrative of 'identity'"[21] since the images it does allow to emerge remain unreadable and hence unrepresentable; it makes narrative impossible. Benjamin's *jetzseit* cannot be identified; it is not a consciousness or "mind"; it *is* not. And although Bhabha clearly problematizes Anderson's schema, as we have seen, his reading of Benjamin's interruptive *jetzseit* also depends on a notion of representation in order to be sustained.[22] Questions remain, therefore, regarding the critical status of those texts that can be localized neither within traditional national narratives, nor as their negative other; that is, as counter-narratives that necessarily depend on the discourses they are attempting to defy or resist. In other words, can the singularity of literary and cultural texts be read without the parallel gesture of identifying them and, therefore, re-inscribing those localizations they themselves do not produce?

Drawing on the important work of postcolonial criticism, recent studies on globalization, transnationalism, and the postnational attempt to think through a critical practice that presupposes that national sovereignty no longer provides the geographical or cultural parameters within or from which to read cultural texts. The New French Studies and the New American Studies, for example, reject or disavow the verticalism and totalizing structures that the thought and narratives of the metropolis (France and the United States in these cases) have imposed on those peoples excluded from traditional national narratives. Emphasis on globalization or the postnational is thus seen as a way to counter homogenizing notions of identity, as in conceptions of *francité* or American Exceptionalism.[23]

Postnational narratives would thus differentiate themselves from postcolonial narratives by creating a space of their own, neither as part of traditional narratives nor apart from (but still within) them, as in Bhabha's formulation. In the words of the Americanist critic Donald Pease, "[t]hese acts of narration have neither ratified the sovereign power of the state nor effected the inclusion of stateless persons within preexisting narratives. They have instead materialized the postnational as the internal boundary insisting at the site where stateless individuals have not yet consented to state power and the state has not yet integrated the stateless into its national order . . . these acts of narration take place as the double apartness (and extensive in-betweenness) of state power and peoples apart

from the state."[24] Although there is an effort here to think through
an autonomous cultural production not dependant on definitions of
the nation as vertically imposed by the state (and thus allow for
revolutionary/resistant nationalisms), largely missing from these
formulations is how postnational thought also and necessarily undoes the normalizing and localizing functions of the postcolonial as
well. That is, on the one hand studies on postnational narratives are
still intent on showing how the margins undo the center, thus maintaining the centrality of precisely what is being questioned and supposedly destabilized and, on the other, maintaining the status quo
of those non-metropolitan or marginalized peoples still at the service of that center.

Using the terms that Bhabha employs in his work, one could ask
if counter-narratives can deconstruct their own pedagogical discourse (or recognize their possible intervention in such a discourse). If a postcolonial or postnational narrative can readily be
acknowledged to permanently destabilize traditional national narratives, can it destabilize what these critics call marginalized texts,
minority writing, Third World Literature, etc.: those categories that
preserve the postcolonial as postcolonial? Can non-metropolitan literary and cultural texts be produced without being identified as op-
posed to, within, or outside state/national boundaries? If not, are
these texts destined to be forever shackled to the colonial legacy of
which they are supposedly rid?

Key to my discussion of community and the function of concepts
such as subject and representation is that postnational paradigms,
despite the designation of the "post" as an after or beyond the normalizing concept of nation and, more importantly, despite the mi-
grations, transnational crossings, and even nomadologies that some
of these paradigms presuppose, still posit a place or ground on
which to inscribe the postnational. For Pease, "the term postnational will function in different registers—postnational narratives,
national narrativity, postcolonial narration—that I hope thereafter
to transmute into the variables *grounding its terrain*. It names the
site in-between the nation and the state that is traversed by these
multiple and heterogeneous acts of narration. These narrative activ-
ities inscribe "national peoples" *within a space* that is neither organic nor contractual, neither the origin nor the end of nation, but
in-between the national and these different acts of narration."[25]
Postnational critical paradigms are thus still anchored to the concept of nation, even as they disavow it.[26]

Although clearly wishing to explore the particularity of cultural production free of the chains of the nation state (which marginalizes, ignores or violently excludes segments of the population that do not fit into its imaginary unity), postnational critical paradigms do not sufficiently explore the problem of representation and of the subject. They are therefore still tied to normalizing, pedagogical concepts, even if ideologically these paradigms are clearly in opposition to the strategies of political containment produced by the nation state.

The challenge still remains how to articulate a non-foundationalist and non-essentialist thought of community based on an ethical relation to the other and to the political exigency of a "we." More importantly, how to elaborate forms of community that do not depend on what, in his *Dis-agreement: Politics and Philosophy*, Jacques Rancière calls the police order: the "general order that arranges that tangible reality in which bodies are distributed in governing their appearing, a configuration of occupations and the properties of spaces where these occupations are distributed."[27] If the police order identifies and localizes, structures and legitimizes (it gives everyone a place and a name), overtly or not, then a notion of community that does not participate in the logic of this order, or inadvertently perpetuates it, must be thought.

Recent work in post-Marxist political philosophy and theory responds to many of the same questions that postcolonial, postnational and globalization theories pose regarding notions of community, but does so by putting into question any direct form of representation and by privileging political subjectification instead of identity and the self.[28] In line with this latter approach, "being in common," such as we will employ this notion throughout the following chapters, points to articulations of community that cannot be reduced to substantive positions or as a ground of the social: the common is, therefore, always open to definition. [29] And because "being in common" is, paradoxically, what is both shared (I and you/I am you) and what divides (you are wholly other than me), it cannot take place in a common locus nor by clearly pre-identified social actors (based on nation, class, ethnic, or even linguistic belonging).[30]

As we will see, this thought of community affects critical discourse in that its articulation can only come about as excessive in relation to the theoretical. If theory's desire is to reign in, delimit, and define its object of study, being in common is precisely what exceeds the horizon of representation. For this reason, "being in common" is essentially poetic because it makes possible the un-foreseeable event—a constant reconfiguration (troping) of senses which, for Rancière, is central to articulating a radical democratic politics: "To affirm the 'poetic' nature in politics means first and foremost that politics is an activity of reconfiguration of that which is given to the sensible."[31] Literary and cultural texts therefore offer important insights into articulations of community not tied to sedimented forms of identity and representation.

IDENTITY AND REPRESENTATION IN LATIN AMERICAN CULTURE

In his *Transculturación narrativa en América Latina* [*Narrative Transculturation in Latin America*], Angel Rama shows that the concept of representation has been a guiding principle in Latin America's literary and cultural production since Independence. This may serve to explain the proliferation of texts where the individual is the central character in accounts of the nation's development, crises, and desires and where the organizing principle is the definition of "el ser nacional." This term can be translated as "national being" or "national subject" (what we think of when defining a citizen), but it also denotes an ontological dimension that makes that national subject a transcendent one.[32] The individual, as a metonymic cipher of the nation, figures in such early works as Domingo Faustino Sarmiento's *Facundo*, as well as in later texts, such as Raúl Scalabrini Ortiz's *El hombre que está sólo y espera* (1931) and Samuel Ramos's *Perfil del hombre y la cultura en México* (1934).[33] In these texts identity is a future-oriented goal, as well as essentializing and ahistorical.

It is because of Latin America's need to become independent from its colonial past, both politically and culturally, that, according to Rama, originality and representativity (the "uniqueness" we discussed above) became the operative terms for cultural production: "o lo creamos o erramos" [either we create it or we err], in the words of Simón Rodriguez.[34] Following Rama, Julio Ramos observes that literature becomes the medium through which a nascent nineteenth-century Latin America could be both defined and expressed. The exemplary case of José Martí attests the fact that literature was the place where Latin America's identity and unity could be represented:

Opuesta a los saberes "técnicos" y a los lenguajes "importados" de la
política oficial la literatura se postula como la única hermenéutica capaz
de resolver los enigmas de la identidad latinoamericana. Martí solía
decir que no habría literatura hasta que no existiese América Latina.
Si la identidad no es desde siempre un dato externo al discurso que lo
nombra—si la forma, la autoridad y el peso institucional del sujeto que
la designa determinan en buena medida el recorte, la selección de los
materiales que componen la identidad—acaso hoy podríamos decir, re-
cordando a Martí, que no habría Latinoamérica hasta que no hubiese un
discurso autorizado para nombrarla. La literatura cargaría con el enorme
y a veces imponente peso de esa *representatividad*.[35]

[Opposed to "technical" knowledge and the "imported" languages of
official politics, literature posits itself as the only hermeneutics capable
of resolving the enigmas of Latin American identity. Martí used to say
that there would be no literature until Latin America existed. If identity
is always external to the discourse that names it—if the form, the authority, and the institutional weight of the subject who designates it determine in great measure the selection of the materials that make up an
identity—perhaps today we could say, remembering Martí, that there
would be no Latin America until there was a discourse authorized to
name it. Literature would carry the enormous and at times imposing
weight of that representation.]

In Martí's Latin America, nation and literature are key elements in
a desire for specularity that in the first half of the twentieth century
will already begin to wane. Although Rama insists that in the period
1910–1940 representation and originality are still the guiding paradigms for literary production, developments in the technologies of
reproduction seriously put in doubt literature's ability to represent
the nation.

In the 1940s the phenomenon of technical reproducibility complicates the earlier model by questioning whether community can
be written at all. The question now becomes if the image produced
by the mass media is not displacing the representational possibilities of the written word. The political dimension of literature thus
moves away from the concept of representation, a move that will
have direct implications on the almost parallel place it held with the
concept of culture.

The problem of representation is nowhere more pronounced than
in discussions on the proper role of language. In a 1927 conference
titled "El idioma de los argentinos" [The language of the Argen-

tines], Borges rejects the "buen decir" [correct speech] of the
Gramática de la Academia Española [*Grammar of the Spanish
Academy*]. It is a useless tool for the Argentinean writer, Borges
says:

> La riqueza del español es el otro nombre eufemístico de su muerte. Abre
> el patán y el no es patán nuestro diccionario y se queda maravillado
> frente al sin fin de voces que están en él y que no están en ninguna
> boca.[36]

> [The richness of Spanish is another euphemistic name for its death. A
> boor and a non-boor open our dictionary and are left marveling at the
> great number of voices that are in the dictionary but are in no one's
> mouth.]

Borges clearly disregards Andrés Bello's pronouncement that "La
gramática de una lengua es el arte de hablarla correctamente"[37]
[The grammar of a language is the art of speaking it correctly] and,
therefore, the only normative principle to maintain the national
unity of an ever more disparate America. And he also distances
himself from the Adamic task that Martí assigns to literature, that of
being able to name and in naming constitute self and place—Latin
America as literature's specular double.

Borges's texts force us to consider the question of the singularity
of what we call Latin American texts. If in spite of the aporias that
constitute the quests of identity, all such quests are inscribed within
an economy that depends on the prior definition of the grounds on
which that quest is possible and if the positing of those grounds
(whether as home, critical substratum, representation, etc.) is precisely what maintains the quest paradigm intact, then an interruption of the quest would allow for their singularity in the removal of
grounds, in the figures of otherness, of excess, of translation and
disorder—what cannot be incorporated into an economy of representation. The term "Latin American" cannot and should not be
done away with, but singularity will be exposed only when the texts
we read are not restricted to an already-established cultural definition.

This is certainly a difficult idea to accept because as critics our
discourse is authorized precisely by the hermeneutic frame we at-
tach to our object of study, but it is precisely in the impossibility of
naming, of defining, of delimiting, that community is exposed. This

is what Maurice Blanchot has called the unavowable community, one which is incomplete, which can never achieve communion, and which never posits itself as the end itself. The unavowable community allows for inventions of collectivity not tied to already sedimented forms or as a response to the failure or loss of aesthetic or political programs. This "other" notion of the collective is not a demystified community, one that is more inclusive or diverse. Instead, it signals the opening to being in common where the "in" no longer functions as a way to localize and fix where the communal is to take place, but to mark the limit of all such localizations and, therefore, the possibilities and imaginings of what is to come.[38]

Texts by Alejo Carpentier, Octavio Paz, Ezequiel Martínez Estrada, and Jorge Luis Borges, principally from the 1940s and '50s, are the focus of *Being in Common*. During this period, these writers confront a world torn apart by two world wars, by the effects of European fascism, by massive political and social changes in Latin America, as well as by the disruption of the epistemological and hermeneutic certainties that the developing mass media are putting into effect. Speaking of the Latin American novel during this period, Jean Franco notes how the concept of nation begins to wane as an interpretive framework: "Individual and collective identity . . . were like shells from which life had disappeared."[39] The 1940s and '50s, therefore, present a decisive historical period in which to study how Latin American writers re-think the notion of community once recourse to traditional paradigms is perceived as no longer being valid.

The emphasis on this historical period allows me to complicate readings where Latin American cultural history is suspended between a teleological discourse of modernity and a postmodern globalization, following Anglo-American and Continental theories that date the collapse of the grand narratives of modernity as a post Cold War phenomenon. Ernesto Laclau summarizes the chronology to which I am referring: "the end of the Cold War has been the end of the globalizing ideologies that had dominated the political arena since 1945 . . . in a post-Cold War world . . . we are witnessing a proliferation of particularistic political identities, none of which tries to ground its legitimacy and its action in a mission predetermined by universal history . . . Any kind of universal grounding is contemplated with deep suspicion."[40] The writers I study put in question this historical framework since, already in the 1940s and 1950, they offer articulations of community that interrupt the totalizing and often violent homogeneity of identity (or difference), the priority of the Subject and the location of culture. However, not simply anchored in a negative epistemology, the texts under discussion are attentive to the singularity of historical experience and thus offer positive articulations of community. In other words, they explore ways of being in common (the communal relation) when the notion of a common being (a totalizing conception of community) is shown to be untenable. The texts discussed in *Being in Common* respond to the following questions: how should art (or the aesthetic) be thought after the violence that the fascist notion of community produced in Europe and in its vernacular forms; what should the role of the writer or intellectual be when the magisterial (pedagogical) role he had been ascribed since the nineteenth century is shown to be no longer viable; and, finally, how can community still be written when the effects of the mass media and the centrality of the image put in doubt the very possibility of narration?

Often still read as either proponents of regional or national particularity (Carpentier, Martínez Estrada) or cosmopolitan universality (Paz, Borges), these writers undo static and binary notions for thinking the ethical and political dimension of literature and culture. In so doing, they also erode the internal coherence of different spheres of knowledge. For this reason, I read their texts as "paradisciplinary" because in their displacement of the concepts that have served to regulate knowledge in Latin American texts, they also displace the very disciplinary (and disciplinarian) boundaries by which that knowledge is communicated. In this way they reformulate the relations between aesthetics and politics.

Given its status as the quintessential text on the Latin American quest of identity and even as the arch-fiction of twentieth-century literary production, Alejo Carpentier's *Los pasos perdidos* [*The Lost Steps*] is the focus of chapter 1, "Writing Place Names: Travel and Theory in Alejo Carpentier's *Los pasos perdidos*." This chapter provides the "road map" for a discussion of the aporias of the quest of identity paradigm, as well as for the relations between travel and theory. In this novel, the narrator's wish to rediscover the authenticity he no longer finds in his own world is constantly and permanently undermined by the traveling which the theory is supposed to uphold, a traveling that makes the theory possible, but which at the same time precludes any notion of immediacy.

Chapter 2, "Image, History, Tradition: Ezequiel Martínez Estrada's Altcr-Nations," examines how the mass media, which rapidly developed during the 1940s and '50s in Argentina (print media, but also film, radio, and photography), begin to erode notions of originality and uniqueness, as well as the temporalities that sustain the concepts of tradition and memory, those elements making up the framework for positing the People as One. Long considered one of the most important Latin American writers of the essay of national identity [ensayo del ser nacional], Martínez Estrada paradoxically discovers the impossibility of maintaining intact the concepts which had served to define the outlines of the Argentinean nation decades earlier and advocates the need to sketch out other forms of the collective.

Chapter 3, "On Being Mexican, for Example: Octavio Paz and the Dialectics of Universality," shows that Paz's texts on Mexican "identity," as well as on poetry, are irreducible to place, politics, or poetics. In his famous essay *El laberinto de la soledad*, Paz articulates how community can be thought outside the parameters that have conventionally defined the quest of identity, without erasing or neutralizing the singularity of being Mexican. This inquiry is also extended to the question of poetry, to the role it occupies in society and to whether it can or should be the "voice" of the community.

Chapter 4, "Borges: On Reading, Translation, and the Impossibility of Naming," explores how during the 1930s and 1940s, Borges turned away from a desire to cultivate a language able to represent a national reality, and instead proposed that translation is the only means for expressing any sense of "innovation." However, for Borges translations never communicate any sense; in fact, as we will see, they are not forms of communication at all. Instead, translations expose the disparities and gaps within and across languages in a never-ending game of mis-naming, of missing the mark. If for Borges there is an Argentinean literature (which is not national), it is one that cannot define itself and cannot define its place, but which paradoxically gives a tenuous "sense" of space, although one that is not localizable. "Concluding Remarks" show how Borges "enacts" being in common as a practice of writing and as a model for the act of reading literary and cultural texts.

1
Writing Place Names: Travel and Theory in Alejo Carpentier's *Los pasos perdidos*

> I should have liked to live in the age of *real* travel, when the spectacle on offer had not yet been blemished, contaminated, and confounded. The alternative is inescapable: either I am a traveler in ancient times, and faced with a prodigious spectacle which would be almost entirely unintelligible to me . . . or I am a traveler of our own day, hastening in search of a vanished reality . . . I am the victim of a double infirmity: what I see is an affliction to me; and what I do not see, a reproach.
> —Claude Lévi-Strauss, *Tristes Tropiques*

> Writing was at its origin the voice of an absent person; and the dwelling-house was a substitute for the mother's womb, the first lodging, for which in all likelihood man still longs, and in which he was safe and felt at ease.
> —Sigmund Freud, *Civilization and its Discontents*

LÉVI-STRAUSS'S "DOUBLE INFIRMITY" IN *TRISTES TROPIQUES* IS A taunting reminder of the limits of his role as an anthropologist and the acknowledgement that his voyage will ultimately be a failed one. Travel confounds all hermeneutics because there can never be *real* travel; all voyages, as we saw in the introduction, are inscribed within an aporetic relation: they require, even demand an expansive and errant discourse, one which promises an endless opportunity for the progressive accumulation of knowledge, while simultaneously needing to anchor that discourse, to limit and identify it.

It is not unusual to find, for this reason, that in many Latin American texts (both criticism and fiction) that thematize the question of travel, the colonial explorations and conquests of the New World are an inevitable reference point, given that the chronicles and letters of Christopher Columbus and Hernán Cortés enact the performative dilemmas of all subsequent travel narratives or quests of identity. For many Latin American writers and critics the "foundational" moment of Latin American history therefore becomes the condition of possibility for the region's contemporary cultural and literary production. Not only because European expansion gave rise to what we presently call Latin America, but because Latin American culture is said, depending on the perspective, to constitute itself in the repetition, disavowal, or overcoming of that errant "foundation."[1]

This is the thesis advanced by Alejo Carpentier in a 1975 speech on the baroque and marvelous realism in which the Cuban writer declares that the muteness to which Cortés was relegated when first encountering America has been overcome by the Latin American writer:

Pero ante los futuros hechos insólitos de ese mundo de lo real maravilloso que nos esperan, no habremos de decir ya, como Hernán Cortés a su monarca: "Por no saber poner los nombres a las cosas no las expreso." Hoy conocemos los nombres de las cosas, las formas de las cosas, la textura de las cosas nuestras: sabemos dónde están nuestros enemigos internos y externos; nos hemos forjado un lenguaje apto para expresar nuestras realidades, y el acontecimiento que nos venga al encuentro hallará en nosotros, novelistas de América Latina, los testigos, cronistas e intérpretes de nuestra gran realidad latinoamericana.[2]

[But faced with the astounding facts of that future world of marvelous reality that awaits us, we need not say, like Hernán Cortés to his monarch: "Because I do not know how to give names to things I will not express them." Today we know the names of things, the forms of things, the texture of our things; we know where our internal and external enemies are; we have forged a language appropriate to express our realities, and the events that we shall encounter will find in us, the novelists of Latin America, the witnesses, chroniclers, and interpreters of our great Latin American reality.]

The baroque and marvelous realism, which throughout this essay are defined as complementary terms, would thus be the expressions of a continent that can no longer be tamed or conquered; which rebels against all types of law, precepts, and institutions.[3] More importantly, in these American expressions, to paraphrase José Lezama Lima, words and things finally coincide. If the colonizers and conquerors had to resort to analogies and comparisons to European models when faced with American reality, or even to muteness, as in the case of Cortés, the revolutionary force of Latin American literature lies in narrating a continent which coincides with itself, where the mimetic force of words makes expression transparent and, therefore, genuinely American.

It would seem, given the description Carpentier offers of the Latin American writer's task as the chronicler, witness, or interpreter of Latin America's marvelous reality, that his quest has finally come to an end and the desired identity localized. In other words, that the aporias that inhabit all quests have been resolved. The theories Carpentier offers on marvelous realism and the baroque intend to put an end to the need to travel. The inversion of Cortés's impossibility to speak when faced with American reality finds its realization in the baroque proliferation of words or an expansive architectural ornamentation, where all empty spaces are filled. The American baroque as counter-conquest, in Carpentier's formulation, rewrites Latin America's foundations as self-constituted; it is the "spirit" and "consciousness" of being American; it is home itself.

Carpentier first established a relation between travel and theory in the preface to *El reino de este mundo* [*The Kingdom of this World*] (1949), later incorporated into the 1975 essay we discussed earlier. A trip taken to Haiti in 1943 allows Carpentier to posit marvelous realism as an essential component of American life. In order to define this notion of marvelous realism, he contraposes it to the literary experiments of the vanguard (especially those of the surrealists) which, according to Carpentier, use a false and contrived technique for problematizing the notion of the real. "[M]e vi llevado a acercar la maravillosa realidad recién vivida a la agotante pretensión de suscitar lo maravilloso que caracterizó a ciertas literaturas europeas de estos últimos treinta años." [I was forced to compare the marvelous reality recently experienced to the exhausting pretension of provoking the marvelous, which characterized certain European literatures of the last thirty years].[4]

Marvelous realism is defined in terms of a dichotomous distinction between art (associated with artifice, Europe, falseness, and the a-historical) and life, which in Carpentier's schema is properly historical and, above all, American. This dichotomous distinction between art and life, between nature and artifice, a distinction problematized by the poetic projects of the vanguard that Carpentier criticizes (and to which he fully subscribed years earlier) relegates art to a (falsely) mimetic and foreign product unable to capture, in a non-mediated fashion, the authentic and originary elements of life.[5]

Following Carpentier's lead, *Los pasos perdidos* [*The Lost Steps*] (1953) is the novel that Latin American critics most often read as emblematic of the continent's quest of identity, as well as a proclamation of an autonomous American reality. When placed within the context of Latin American literary and cultural production of the 1940s and 50s and its concern with defining and delimiting a properly American history and tradition (distinct from Europe), *Los pasos perdidos* seems to have much in common with works such as Fernando Ortiz's *Contrapunteo cubano del tabaco y el azúcar* [*Cuban Counterpoint of Tobacco and Sugar*] (1940) and Pedro Henríquez Ureña's *Las corrientes literarias en la América Hispana* [*Literary Currents in Spanish America*] (1949). Carpentier's narrator also seems to discover an autonomous Latin America with its own history (traceable to its very origin), customs, and traditions, a primordial Latin America imbued with an authenticity he no longer finds in his own world. In this novel Latin America is a pure and utopic place out of time, a stark contrast to both a Europe grown decadent and immoral (an "antro del horror" [cave of horror]) in the aftermath of the Second World War, and a North America deemed artificial and mechanical (the novel indicates that the narrator lives in New York).[6]

However, *Los pasos perdidos* fits uncomfortably within the genealogy proposed above since it defies both the theories that Carpentier himself had earlier proposed concerning the role and function of Latin American literature and the Latin American writer, as well as the critical discussions that place the novel within the continent's quest of identity. In this novel, what at first appears to be a journey back to the source of Latin American history and culture will be constantly and inevitably undermined by the traveling which the theory is supposed to uphold, a traveling that makes the theory possible, but which at the same time precludes any notion of immediacy.

The difficulties that the narrator encounters in writing Latin America (and I omit the prepositions "about" or "on" deliberately in order to foreground the narrator's project to found it anew and, in a writing that pretends to erase its mediating function, name Latin American reality), will frustrate not only the aesthetic project he presents in the novel. Those difficulties also point to the limits and limitations of theorizing Latin America. In fact, *Los pasos perdidos* poses a series of questions that are crucial for literary and cultural criticism: why travel if the destination is already known or at least surmised; can one travel without knowing when the traveling will stop? What would such a notion of travel entail and would we still be able to call it a critical enterprise? In other words, can literary and cultural criticism think beyond the notion of place that an object of study, as object, seems to demand?

In *Alejo Carpentier, The Pilgrim at Home*, Roberto González Echevarría notes that the narrator's failed quest for authenticity in *Los pasos perdidos* functions as a "response" to the poetic project put forth in the preface to *El reino de este mundo*. *Los pasos perdidos* would thus come to show that the role ascribed by Carpentier to the Latin American artist is impossible to achieve.[7] González, as well as other critics, explain the narrator's "failure" in terms of the dichotomy that Carpentier himself establishes in the preface: the lack of immediacy implied in the act of writing.[8] Writing (understood to be the narrator's account of his travels) is what stands in the way of his unmediated access to what is natural, immediate, and true. It is the destiny as well as the defeat of the modern artist. This notion of writing presupposes a relation of secondariness to that which is most authentic or original and forms part of a long tradition in Western literature since Plato.[9] Writing thus becomes the culprit in an enterprise that would have succeeded "if only. . . ."

Critical discussions of *Los pasos perdidos* place the novel within the framework of the American baroque, marvelous realism, or as part of the Latin American Boom of the 1960s, although the novel was published in 1953. Read within the context of these literary histories, *Los pasos perdidos* would be, in the first and second cases, the overcoming of the constrictions that the language of the colonizer imposed on the expression of American reality or, in the third, the compensatory positing of a continental literary identity in the face of a modernization that threatens to do away with the very place of the literary. In all these versions, the affirmation of an American identity is read as aprés-coup, mournful, since they point to a plenitude that is always already lost.

Yet what is not expressed in these readings is that in *Los pasos perdidos* the theory that is supposed to uphold the narrative can never be fulfilled, the narrator cannot physically, literally, identify the road that will allow his entry to the origin: the pre-fallen, premodern Latin American world. In this novel Latin America cannot be a sign to be read and deciphered. And because the narrator cannot become the Adamic hero/writer of these critical narratives, the place of the literary, and more specifically of writing, remains a problem, as well as the placement of this novel within the cultural aspirations of the Boom and the baroque. In other words, if the literary in *Los pasos perdidos* does not serve to ground identity, then Carpentier, surely in spite of himself, is proposing another way to think the relation between writing and theory, as well as how the notion of culture is imbricated in that relation.

SIGN LANGUAGE

In *Los pasos perdidos* the narrator rehearses the different discursive modalities that the economy of travel may take. For this reason, his narrative is by turn that of a tourist, a discoverer, an adventurer, an ethnologist, a novelist, and a journalist. As I indicated in the introduction, the concept of travel functions by positing a transcendental place, the home, which operates as the point of origin and of return. This place ensures that the economy of travel will be sustained and that any wandering or errancy that may occur will be accounted for.

The novel begins the first day of the narrator's vacation and the traveling is that of a tourist. A chance meeting with the curator of the museum provides the narrator with the solution as to how to occupy his free time: "la tarea encomendada podía ser llevada a buen término en el tiempo de mis vacaciones" [the job in question could be easily done during my vacation.][10] The economy of tourism can be seen to follow the economy of travel that I discussed earlier. In fact, when Mouche (the narrator's lover and traveling companion) first suggests obtaining "fake" instruments for the curator (in order not to have to reach the jungle to get them), the idea is first accepted and then rejected by the narrator:

No seguiríamos viviendo la estafa imaginada por mi amiga . . . Lo más sencillo, lo más limpio. . . . era emplear el tiempo de las vacaciones que me quedaba cumpliendo con el Curador y con la Universidad, llevando a cabo, honestamente, la tarea encomendada. (199)

[We would not go on living with the hoax imagined by my friend. . . . The simplest, the most decent, the most interesting thing to do would be to keep faith with the Curator and with the university, carrying out the mission I had been assigned.]

When at the end of the novel the narrator states, "Hoy terminaron las vacaciones de Sísifo" [Today Sisyphus' vacation came to an end] (414), one is again reminded that the economy of travel is the novel's theoretical, as well as ideological framework from the beginning to the final page of the novel. As we will see, the fact that this economy is sustained throughout the novel is important in order to understand the aporias of the quest of identity and the relation between travel and theory.

Los pasos perdidos explores the consequences of the economy of travel by engaging with one of its earliest literary examples: Homer's *The Odyssey*. Odysseus is the very figure of the traveler in Western literature: he leaves his home on a voyage of self-awareness, knowledge, and glory and, after many trials and death-threatening experiences, returns to reclaim his home and his wife, Penelope. The narrative tells the story of an initial loss of the home, but this initial loss is later balanced by the home's re-appropriation upon Odysseus's return. The economy is thus a closed circle.

Just like Odysseus, the narrator of *Los pasos perdidos* also sets out on a voyage of discovery (of self and others); he is a broken man of reason who must go through a series of trials in order to show his strength and fortitude while traveling through the jungle.[11] The relation with Homer's text is also reinforced thematically: Yannes, the Greek miner, gives the narrator a copy of *The Odyssey* as a token of their friendship and the latter then decides to compose a threnody based on Homer's text. Further, if the *Odyssey* can be said to be the trials and experiences of a man who only wishes to return home, then the narrator's journey in *Los pasos perdidos* mimics the presuppositions of the Greek text. Although the narrator travels because he believes his modern, city life to be inauthentic, he embarks on a journey not to displace the notion of home, but to better define it. He wishes to find a more genuine, true home, one in which wandering will no longer be either desired or needed; that is, where the traveling will stop.

Much like the Adelantado in Santa Mónica de los Venados, the narrator also wishes to be a founder, to domesticate the jungle and establish a home:

> Fundar una ciudad. Yo fundo una ciudad. Él ha fundado una ciudad. Es posible conjugar semejante verbo. Se puede ser Fundador de una ciudad. Crear y gobernar una ciudad que no figure en los mapas, que se sustraiga a los horrores de la época, que nazca así, de la voluntad de un hombre, en este mundo del Génesis. (322)

[To found a city. I found a city. He has founded a city. It is possible to conjugate such a verb. One can be the founder of a city. To create and govern a city that does not appear in maps, that is distanced from the horrors of this age, that is born from the will of one man, in this world of Genesis.]

In order to achieve his goal, the narrator decides to marry Rosario so as to establish, much like Odysseus, the economy of the home with Penelope as its center; it is Penelope who secures the propriety and property of the home by rejecting the suitors (usurpers), thus guaranteeing that Odysseus will be able to re-appropriate it upon his return. The domestication of the woman thus becomes a way to stop the traveling and ensure the sexual difference needed to keep the concept of home intact.

The novel constantly problematizes the differences between founding and finding, given that the positing of an origin requires a process of localization: the home marks the very beginning and end of meaning. As the epigraph from Freud that opens this chapter suggests, the home (dwelling house) is traditionally read as a substitute for the mother's womb and, for this reason, Rosario's function in the narrator's aesthetic project is critical. Rosario provides the narrator with the chance of a more authentic homing than what he experienced with his wife Ruth and thus the possibility of having founding and finding coincide.[12] However, this coincidence proves to be unrealizable given Rosario's refusal to become the narrator's Penelope.

When at the end of the novel the narrator asks about the whereabouts of Rosario, Yannes tells him that she has married Marcos, the Adelantado's son, and will soon have his child: "Ella no Penélope" [She not Penelope] (412). This last affirmation is crucial because, as one recalls from the Homerian text, Penelope guarantees the very possibility of Odysseus's return: the domesticated home that provides the point of reference for his voyage. Penelope must be the one to recognize Odysseus upon his return in order to assure, to verify, and thus to authenticate the identity of the stranger who calls himself her husband. In order to do so, Penelope asks a series of questions that Odysseus must answer in order to be certain she has received the "sure signs," signs which would make words and things coincide and (literally) re-establish a lost presence.[13]

Unlike Odysseus, the narrator of *Los pasos perdidos* cannot give "sure signs," much less read them, as he is something of a failed

semiologist. On his return to the jungle, it is precisely his inability
to read the sign (the three Vs engraved on the tree trunk that should
provide the entry into Santa Mónica de los Venados) that impedes
him from culminating his voyage to the jungle as a voyage to the
source, to the origin: his own and Latin America's. The sign that
would deliver him back "home" remains elusive, hidden, secret:

> Con la vista fija en los troncos, busco, a la altura del pecho de un hom-
> bre que estuviera de pie sobre el agua, la incisión que dibuja tres V
> superpuestas verticalmente, en un signo que pudiera alargarse hasta el
> infinito . . . Pero pongo tanta atención en mirar, en no dejar de mirar, en
> pensar que miro, que al cabo de un momento mis ojos se fatigan de ver
> pasar constantemente el mismo tronco. Me asaltan dudas de *haber visto*
> sin darme cuenta; me pregunto si no me habré distraído durante algunos
> segundos; mando volver atrás, y sólo encuentro una mancha clara sobre
> una corteza o un simple rayo de sol. (404)

> [With my eyes riveted on the trees, I watch for the three V's one above
> the another, at the height of a man's breast if he were standing on the
> water . . . But I pay so much attention to looking, to looking so closely,
> to thinking that I am looking, that after some time my eyes become
> weary of seeing the same tree. I begin to wonder if I have seen without
> realizing it; I ask myself if I have not become distracted during a few
> seconds, I order him to turn back and only find a clear spot on a tree
> truck or a simple ray of light.]

There seems to be something that defies identification in America
and even that defies the act of interpreting itself.[14] For this reason,
the narrator's quest for authenticity is at odds with the theories he
espouses concerning his role as a Latin American writer: "compre-
nderlo todo, anotarlo todo, explicar en lo posible" [to understand
everything, to note everything down, to explain it, if possible]
(342).[15] Indeed, the scene of the three Vs condenses the aporias
present in the quest of identity itself. The voyage into Santa Mónica
de los Venados, which promises to be the narrator's final voyage,
the one that will put to rest the desire to travel itself becomes instead, as the citation indicates, a scene of back and forth move-
ments and of distractions. This final voyage, which should make
travel and theory coincide, thus supplying the narrator with the desired home, is instead deferred and infinitely postponed.

In this scene, the Vs both denote the plenitude that the narrator
searches for (it is therefore the mark of that plenitude) while at the

same time functioning merely as a sign—the mark of an absence, the impossibility of the fulfillment of that plenitude. But of course these three Vs do not allow for an economy of loss and gain to be instituted, given that these marks literally do not mark (they are below water) and, therefore, cannot be found or identified. Indeed, the marks that the narrator cannot see suggest that they do not belong to the order of the phenomenal, or to the order of presence.

Mary Louise Pratt rightly states that *Los pasos perdidos* reverses many of the "value signs" of Alexander Von Humboldt's invention of America, his unabashed and imperial meaning-making. In Carpentier's novel, the narrator's description of nature remits to "a plenitude not of discovery but of unknowability, a world that metropolitan consciousness is unequipped to decipher or embrace."[16] If the marks and signs which are supposed to signify the entry into an authentic Latin American reality cannot be made to signify and cannot fulfill that function because they are also unlocalizable (hidden, secret), then the unity sought for (be this in the form of identity, origin, or even as the possibility for "a new beginning," the possibility for starting the quest once again, although differently) is infinitely deferred. In fact, the verb tenses in this quotation, the oscillation between the present and the past present ("I look," "I search," and "have seen"), destines the search for a Latin American identity to an infinite postponement, to an origin which may never have taken place and for this reason cannot be made present.

Critics of Carpentier have noted that the impossibility of fixing a stable, unambiguous signified to the quest of identity results in the never-ending process of beginning anew. Thus, the search would be destined to a continuous repetition, albeit one not dictated by the logic of the Same; the "new" beginnings would allow for the production of literary fictions that we call Latin American literature. What are the implications and effects of this never-ending "beginning anew"? First, the positing of a foundation, however provisional. That is, a place (a point of origin: whether in-between, at the margins, self-constituted, or referential) which can serve to prescribe and thus define how literary texts are read.[17] Second, and perhaps more importantly, turning the quest into a dialectical one in which the failed quest itself becomes a victory, given that a new truth can be brought forth.

The question remains then of how to read the failed quest of identity and, more importantly, how to determine in a positive manner the resistance of a certain critical discourse to that failure. The scene of the three Vs that I discussed earlier frames the travel narrative retroactively, coming as it does at the end of the novel. Once the scene of the failed quest of identity is read, one must re-travel the route undertaken by the narrator and re-think the concepts which allowed the theory to try to keep pace with the travel. However, does retracing the steps (even the lost steps) imply that our own attempt will be a failure? Or, as we mentioned earlier, that the critical text is destined to repeat the quest? In other words, does re-visiting the concepts which structure the literary text studied mean becoming prey to its own logic; is there no way out of the quest of identity?

In *Los pasos perdidos*, the narrator seeks a re-appropriation of presence through a control of vision, through a certain notion of music, and, consequently, of language. However, in the novel these concepts (vision, music, and language) present their internal limits, the aporias which allow them to unfold as such but which at the same time do not permit them to enjoy their plenitude. It is only by reading these limits that any problematization of hierarchy and order can be approached in this text and thus, ultimately, the relation between travel and theory. This is an important task for a criticism that wishes to avoid re-inscribing or re-semanticizing the very concepts it is questioning. In addition, and simultaneously, these categories are critical for thinking the concept of theory itself. If traveling always exceeds the theory in some way, then we must stop thinking of theory or travel in relation to some fixed place. How would such a criticism be written?

INSIGHT TO BLINDNESS

In the epigraph from Lévi-Strauss which opens this chapter, the act of seeing is proposed as central to the anthropologist's task: to capture the immediacy of what is before him as the experience of an other, even as he acknowledges that sight is an imperfect tool. The scopic regime to which Lévi-Strauss's anthropology belongs privileges sight as a means of attaining knowledge, truth, and meaning. Perception, an activity of the eye, would thus be able to make possible an experience of the immediate and the identity of the actual.[18]

The narrator's notion of the function of vision lies at the heart of the Platonic notion of mimesis. Discussions of mimesis center on

two alternatives for thinking the concept: good and bad mimesis.[19]
In the novel, the problem of good and bad mimesis is problematized
in an almost banal and dichotomous fashion. Bad mimesis is associated with Ruth's theater world, as well as with the ridiculed Latin
American artists the narrator meets at the Canadian woman's house
when escaping from the revolution (these artists wish to imitate the
latest Parisian trend without paying the least attention to the reality
that surrounds them). Yet there is a good mimesis in the novel that
is developed most fully in the narrator's musical project (and will
be discussed below) but is first presented through the question of
vision. Vision for the narrator is part of the process of good mimesis where the copy (the word) has a natural and direct relation to
the original model: it is the desire for plenitude itself.

In *Los pasos perdidos* vision is at the heart of the narrator's project as a voyage to the source. In fact, before the sixth and final
chapter of the novel, the success of that project is presented in visual terms:

> Lo que he visto confirma . . . la tesis de quienes dijeron que la música
> tiene un origen mágico. Pero ésos llegaron a tal razonamiento a través
> de los libros . . . yo, en cambio he visto, cómo la palabra emprendía su
> camino hacia el canto. (333)

> [What I have seen confirms . . . the thesis of those who have said that
> music has a magical origin. But they have reached that conclusion
> through the study of books . . . I, on the other hand, have seen how the
> word began its journey toward song.]

Vision in *Los pasos perdidos* not only serves to prove the truth of
an experience or theory; it is also the very essence of existence and
therefore foundational: vision is creation and is at the heart of signification: "Lo hecho no acababa de estar hecho mientras otro no lo
mirara. Pero bastaba que uno solo lo mirara para que la cosa fuera,
y se hiciera creación verdadera por la mera palabra de un Adán
nombrando" [What was done was not truly done until someone
looked at it. It was enough for someone to look at it for the thing to
exist and be a true creation because of the mere word of a Naming
Adam] (376).

This mimetic notion of language, where words merely "mirror"
thoughts as a vehicle of signification is, however, also put in doubt
in the novel. When commenting on the plants in the jungle which
the Fraile shows him, the narrator states:

Inclinado sobre el caldero demoníaco, me siento invadido por el vértigo de los abismos; sé que si me dejara fascinar *por lo que aquí veo*, mundo de lo prenatal, de *lo que existía cuando no había ojos*, acabaría por arrojarme, por hundirme, en ese tremendo espesor de hojas que desaparecerán del planeta, un día, sin haber sido nombradas, sin haber sido recreadas por la Palabra." (338, italics mine)

[Leaning over the bedeviled caldron, I felt the vertigo of the abyss. I know that if I let myself come under the spell of what *I am seeing here*, this prenatal world, *of what existed before there were eyes*, I would hurl myself down, burying myself in this tremendous density of leaves that will one day disappear from the planet, without having been given a name, without having been re-created by the Word. Italics mine]

What exists from a time when there were no eyes (when things could not be seen) thus threatens to do away with the experience of the immediate that the narrator seeks. As in the scene of the three Vs, there seems to be something supplemental in the jungle that disrupts the narrator's search for self-presence and origins. The ability to see is thus at the beginning of words, but also at their end; the eyes are birth and death. This defeat of vision (of vision and by vision) is most clear at the end of the narrator's quest, when he searches for the sign that will provide his entry into Santa Mónica de los Venados. The three Vs that mark the final defeat in the narrator's quest of a Latin American identity are a taunting reminder that those signs are outside his perception. The three "ves" ("you see" in Spanish) are precisely what he cannot see.

In the scene of the three Vs, vision is prey to a vertiginous play of mirrors that threaten to undo the very notion of mimesis and of representation. In that scene the three letters vertically superimposed one inside the other seem to repeat themselves to infinity in much the same way as the experience of the narrator in the cavelike jungle passage which is to return him to Santa Mónica de los Venados:

[a]l cabo de algún tiempo de navegación en aquel caño secreto, se producía un fenómeno parecido al que conocen los montañeses extraviados en las nieves: se perdía la noción de la verticalidad, dentro de una suerte de desorientación, de mareo de los ojos. No se sabía ya lo que era del árbol y lo que era del reflejo. No se sabía ya si la claridad venía de abajo o de arriba. (291–92)[20]

[After sailing for some time through that secret channel, one began to feel the same thing that mountain climbers feel, lost in the snow: the loss of the sense of verticality, a kind of disorientation, and a dizziness of the eyes. It was no longer possible to say which was tree and which reflection of tree. Was the light coming from above or below?]

This *mise en abyme* sequence is repeated throughout the novel so that the Latin American reality that the narrator says to be presenting "for the first time" can only be seen as itself a reproduction: the narrator describes scenes in the jungle as theater, as well as simulacra. In the sequence of the petroglyphs, the narrator sees traces and marks that denote the figures of scorpions, birds, and other signs that he cannot understand. Yet the explanation the Adelantado gives him is "una explicación inesperada" ["an unexpected explanation"] because those signs which supposedly denote a reality unlike his own tell the story of the Deluge and Noah's Ark. With some variations they tell, as the Adelantado notes, "los mismos cuentos" [the same stories] (329). The narrator accepts the explanation given to him but the ambiguity remains as to whether he accepts them as stories or lies, since in Spanish "the same stories" can refer to both. The final irony of the scene of the petroglyphs of course is that the signs and marks he sees with the Adelantado prefigures his inability to read the three Vs toward the end of the novel. That is, he sees but does not understand a writing which does not succumb to a watery grave, but is unable to see the signs which are supposed to coincide with the meaning of his voyage, the quest of identity.

NATURE'S MUSIC

The question of Nature and of what can be considered to be natural (authentic, original, unsullied) in the novel is developed in relation to music, a problematic that figures in many of Carpentier's texts.[21] Carpentier was familiar with Jean Jacques Rousseau's writings, including those on music where the French philosopher sets forth the theory that there is no music before language.[22] In fact, for Rousseau, music is born at the same time as words; they are an expression of passions and thus mark the beginning of human society. In the novel, the narrator seeks to replicate this theory in the musical composition that he begins to write in the jungle, a threnody based on Homer's *The Odyssey*:

Yo buscaba . . . una expresión musical que surgiera de la palabra des-
nuda, de la palabra anterior a la música. . . . y que pasara de lo hablado
a lo cantado de modo casi insensible, el poema haciéndose música . . .
Yo había imaginado una suerte de cantata, en que un personaje con fun-
ciones de corifeo se adelantara hacia el público y, en total silencio de la
orquesta . . . comenzara a decir un poema muy simple, hecho de vo-
cablos de uso corriente, sustantivos como hombre, mujer, casa, agua,
nube, árbol, y otros que por su elocuencia primordial no necesitaran de
adjetivo. Aquello sería como una verbogénesis. (347)

[I was looking for a musical expression that would spring from the
naked word, from the word prior to music . . . that would go from speaking to singing almost insensibly, the poem become music . . . I had
imagined a sort of cantata in which a character taking the role of the
coryphaeus would step forward and, without a sound from the orchestra,
after a gesture to attract the attention of the audience, would begin to
say a very simple poem, made up of common words, nouns like man,
woman, house, water, cloud, tree, and others that because of their primordial eloquence require no adjective. A kind of word-genesis.]

The desire to be present both at the birth of music as well as of
words presupposes a concept of the voice and of speech as the origin of human society. The notion of a transparent and unmediated
relation between world and representation, between words and
things is, of course, at the heart of a notion of mimesis as natural
resemblance. The narrator of *Los pasos perdidos*, in his quest for
a non-mediated relation with the natural primordial world of Latin
America wishes to create music that is nature itself.

The threnody, a musical performance associated with ritual,
magic, and resurrection ("hacer volver un muerto a la vida," 350),
is the medium through which the narrator seeks to bring forth the
desired "word-genesis." It is death, then, that will bring the word
to life and will make it present. In this sense, the narrator's musical
project follows a traditional notion of representation in which the
absent is made present. For this reason, he wishes to use Shelley's
Prometheus Unbound as the model for his threnody: "La liberación
del encadenado, que asocio mentalmente a mi fuga de *allá*, tiene
implícito un sentido de *resurrección, de regreso entre las sombras*,
muy conforme a la concepción original del treno" ["The liberation
of the chained prisoner, which I mentally associated with my flight
from *there*, conveyed a sense of *resurrection, a re-emergence from
among the shadows*, appropriate to the original conception of the

threnody"] (350, italics mine).[23] But as he does not have Shelley's text at hand, the narrator must instead rely on *The Odyssey*. The part of the text that he chooses for the threnody is Book 11 where Odysseus must descend into Hades and speak with the dead, principally the ghost of Teiresias. He will prophesy when Odysseus will be able to return to Ithaca, his home.[24]

Instead of using a text (Shelley's) which will represent the making alive of the voice, thus ensuring the self-presentation of nature, the narrator of *Los pasos perdidos* must rely on a wandering text, the travels of Odysseus, which postpones the making present of his presence, the deferral of his return home. Thus, no return is assured by the threnody (neither his own, nor of the full presence of the voice) but, rather, unending travel. Perhaps this is because travel itself presupposes death or absence. As Van Den Abbeele notes, "[t]ravel is deadly and to be feared to the extent that it raises the possibility of there being no return, but without the possibility of no return (of death), there could be no such thing as travel."[25]

The aporias of the relations between death and travel, presence and absence, music and writing, become evident in a dialogue between the narrator and Rosario, while the former is writing the threnody:

> Y cuando más exasperado me encuentro, Rosario me pregunta a quién estoy escribiendo cartas, puesto que aquí no hay correo. Esa confusión, la imagen de la carta hecha para viajar y que no puede viajar, me hace pensar, de súbito, en la vanidad de todo lo que estoy haciendo desde ayer. De nada sirve la partitura que no ha de ser ejecutada. La obra de arte se destina a los demás, y muy especialmente la música." (357)

> [And when I feel most exasperated, Rosario asks me to whom I am writing letters, because there is no post office here. That confusion, the image of a letter meant to travel and that cannot travel suddenly makes me think about the vanity of all I have been doing since yesterday. A score that is not played is of no value. A work of art is destined for others, especially music.]

The narrator here summarizes the problematic nature of his musical project: either there is travel, accompanied by the danger of death and destruction—the danger that the sought-for presence will not be achieved—or there is no travel and the letter (the text, writing) has no possibility of being able to reach its mark: the theory which the narrator delineates beforehand. This aporia is of course at the heart of the problem of any discourse that seeks to postulate the existence of natural signs. As we saw in the section on vision above, mimetic notions of art, where nature is either model or object, have the makings of their own undoing, as they are inhabited by those very elements which both make them possible and inevitably undermine them. In her postal exchange with the narrator, Rosario intimates that the relations between the music and the letter, between nature and artifice, can exist neither dialectically nor as simple oppositions. Each inhabits the other, undoing its borders and definitions, interrupting all quests for plenitude.

On Naming: No One

As we have seen from the narrator's Adamic project, the desire to name in this novel and by so doing self-name or baptize one who has no name, is an enterprise infinitely sought and yet constantly deferred in the novel. Like Odysseus before the Cyclops in Homer's text, the narrator remains "No one," the unnamed, hence identity-less. But if in *The Odyssey* the protagonist's lack of identity was a ruse to ward off death (it is a survival tactic), one must wonder why the narrator in *Los pasos perdidos* remains nameless, as this situation is at odds with the poetic project which is at the heart of the narrator's quest: to be a "Naming Adam," a creator and giver of names. Birth and death cohabit the name, or its lack, in this novel.

The lack of the narrator's proper name serves various functions in the novel. As many critics have noted, the novel mimics the conventions of autobiography (it is written in the first person) and logically would have no need of a signature, since the text would be destined only for the narrator himself. And yet the purposeful exclusion of the name, the fact that emphasis is placed on the character Rosario calling the narrator by his name as "if for the first time" all put the signature in question. What does the proper name or its lack point to? The proper name is precisely what cannot be described or generalized, that is, what is properly unique. It is meant to be the mark of the pure idiom, the untranslatable, and also what is most proper, what one could call one's own. Yet, as we see throughout the novel, it is precisely the concept of uniqueness (and specifically the uniqueness of Latin America) that is questioned in the novel (it is both affirmed and denied), as well as what is called home, the proper itself.

It is not only himself that the narrator cannot name in the novel, but also the places which are supposed to act as markers of his travel. Indeed, if a traveler or tourist visits a specific site in a "foreign country" it is precisely to emphasize that the site is authentic.[26] And yet the narrator cannot name what he sees; he must resort to circumlocutions (analogies, tropes) in order to "designate" what is in fact impossible to name. Irlemar Chiampi convincingly shows the narrator's "aphasic" response to the American marvelous reality. His many exclamations of "asombro," "estar estupefacto" [astonishment, to be speechless] point to the impossibility of giving name to what he thinks he sees. Like Cortés before him, the narrator repeats the experience of strangeness and the impossibility of representation: "Y aun cuando encontraba una analogía, tenía que renunciar a ella, al punto, por una cuestión de proporciones" [And even when I found an analogy, I had to quickly dismiss it, because of a question of proportions] (155).[27]

That is why it is important that in the postface Carpentier identifies all the places the narrator visits as real precisely because the author had also visited them.[28] Carpentier does so by following the logic of the traveler, tourist, witness, and journalist, that is, through each of the discursive positions performed by the narrator-protagonist of the novel. This unusual postface contradicts the poetic project of the novel by identifying and giving a name to what in the novel could not and would not be named. It is as if Carpentier felt uncomfortable with what his writing had produced and thus sought, if only in a few pages, to legitimate all the strategies by which a pre-modern notion of mimesis could be reestablished in the novel.

Vision, therefore, will once again be acknowledged as the guarantor of a unique Latin American reality: "el paisaje se ciñe a visiones muy precisas de lugares poco conocidos y apenas fotografiados-cuando lo fueron alguna vez" [the landscape conforms to very precise sights of places rarely if ever seen or photographed] (415). Most importantly, in the postface Carpentier reinstates the very hermeneutics that the novel disavowed. In fact, like a good semiologist, he uncovers the secret of the sign: "El paso con la triple incisión en forma de "V" que señala la entrada del paso secreto, existe, efectivamente, con el Signo, en la entrada del Caño de la Guacharaca, situado a unas dos horas de navegación, más arriba del Vichada" [The passage with the triple incision in the form of a V marking the entrance to the secret channel really exists, with the Sign, at the entrance of the Guacharaca Channel, some two hours'

sail up the Vichada] (415). Carpentier's final assertion indicates
that the theory regarding Latin American art that he delineated in
the preface to *El reino de este mundo* is still operating in *Los pasos
perdidos* as the *theoretical* framework of the novel. As I have
shown, however, the narrator's travel always exceeds the theory he
is trying to keep in check.

What is the relation between writing and travel that makes for the
undermining of the theoretical goal of the novel? What effects does
writing (travel) produce that would make a text wander? Travel does
not provide the narrator with any greater notion of immediacy than
that which he finds in the "false" world he wishes to leave behind.
His quest then does not take him any closer to finding the Latin
American identity that he so wishes to discover.

In this chapter I demonstrate the ways in which *Los pasos perdidos* constantly undermines the notion of place needed in order to
define travel and theory. Place is precisely what cannot be found (in
the sense of foundations and of meaning). This is not to say that
Carpentier was inadvertently denying the existence of Latin
America, but rather that writing always misses its mark, although it
is routed and directed. Indeed, although maps and charts are meant
to guide it, there is in writing some thing that exceeds or is less than
what can be called its quest for knowledge or identity, the exposition of ideology or theory. Because it cannot be represented, it
functions "outside" the economy of exchange. We could perhaps
call this "thing" the singularity of the text, and herein lies its resistance to any law or precept, to any boundary that wishes to enclose
and identify it, whether European or Latin American.

2
Image, History, Tradition:
Ezequiel Martínez Estrada's Alter-Nations

Costa de un mar de ignorados dramas y de frustradas
glorias; muelle donde el ser humano deambula sin pasaporte ni
ancla.

[A sea coast of ignored dramas and frustrated glories; a dock
where human beings move aimlessly without passport or an-
chor].
　　　　　—E. Martínez Estrada, *La cabeza de Goliat* [*The Head of Goliath*]

IF D. F. SARMIENTO SAW THE VAST EXPANSE OF LANDS IN THE POST-
colonial Argentina of the mid-1800s and worried about how to fill
that void and, by so doing, literally create a nation, in 1940
Ezequiel Martínez Estrada wanders through a Buenos Aires over-
flowing with people, buildings, and noise and only sees ruins. In *La
cabeza de Goliat* (1940) the city Sarmiento envisioned as the emblem of his political and cultural project becomes, for Martínez Estrada, the symptom of an impossible national unity and even an
example of the type of immanent community produced by Sarmiento's projects: fascism.[1]

In the 1920s and '30s, many writers described the modern Buenos Aires that Martínez Estrada registers in *La cabeza de Goliat*:
its modernity (noise, speed, and heterogeneity, for example) was a
cause for concern and discussion, as Beatriz Sarlo has shown. During this period writers confront a city which is rapidly changing due
to the make-up of its population, as well as because of new forms
of mass communication (movie houses, print media, advertising)
and transportation. The modalities of the writers' responses to "an
aesthetics of the new" are varied, according to Sarlo: Ricardo Güiraldes recreates an "edad dorada" [a golden age], a narrative of uto-
pian rural life not disturbed by changes in demography, where

49

hierarchies are natural and non-changing; Jorge Luis Borges legitimates the margin ("la orilla") in order to produce both local and universal texts; Roberto Arlt creates his fiction out of the knowledge ("los saberes") of the marginalized and the working class, those actors on the urban scene who now become the protagonists of his novels.

Even though writers such as Güiraldes reject the changes brought on by the effects of modernization, the notion of a homogeneous national culture is already considered a problem and writers must present new ways of expressing Argentinean culture as a "cultura de mezcla" [hybrid culture].[2] Yet what is not put in question is that there is a national culture (or cultures) that must be represented; the question simply becomes what forms that representation will take. However, *La cabeza de Goliat* approaches the problem of modernization differently. No longer concerned with finding new ways of expressing the nation, Martínez Estrada wonders if such expression is even possible. That is, can the identity of a nation which, in the words of Martínez Estrada, "undoes itself" ("se deshace") be represented? What cohesion, if any, can be found in the "volumes" of people walking in the street, where should or can that desired unity be located? Further, what should the role of literature, and even of writing, be at this juncture?

La cabeza de Goliat is not Martínez Estrada's first incursion into the problems of national culture and identity. Even though almost total silence greeted the publication of his *Radiografía de la pampa* [*X-Ray of the Pampa*] (1933), Martínez Estrada becomes associated, even to this day, with a hermeneutics proper to the essay of national identity. *Radiografía* proposes to show the wrongs ("los males") which have prevented the nation from developing a proper culture (proper in the sense of unique or original, but also correct and moral) and the desired national unity. Martínez Estrada wishes to prove that the nation's problems are a product of being a bad copy, of suffering "los males de la apariencia" (344) [the errors of appearances] (344).[3] Destined to a second-order imitation (imitating Europe and even Europe's imitations), the nation necessarily becomes a counterfeit reality, a play of pure theater.[4] The notion of copy in *Radiografía* is always that of the resemblance to an original, to what is considered authentic; the essay thus becomes a diagnosis, an X-ray of the pampa, and the radiographer must find "las vísceras y órganos de un cuerpo en tres dimensiones" [the viscera and organs of a body in three dimensions] (62). The origin of the wrongs committed exists and can be discovered and Martínez Estrada ends the essay with the belief that the nation can one day live "unidos en salud" [united in health] (346).

The unity of the nation and the representation of that unity will not be put in doubt until seven years later, with the publication of *La cabeza de Goliat* (1940). This text develops many of the same themes first introduced in the 1933 essay, but with a markedly different hermeneutics.[5] Although still profoundly anchored in a scopic regime mediated by an optical device, the counterfeit reality that was the center of the diagnosis of *Radiografía* gives way to the simulacra of *La cabeza de Goliat*. And if in 1933 the essayist fancied himself a radiographer, a seeker of essences and, therefore, of the meanings of the nation, in 1940 Martínez Estrada is reduced to seeing through a photographic eye, a change which will mark a shift not only in the essayist's ability to posit the truth of the community and the road to its communion, but also to question the very possibility of giving expression or representing what, in 1940, already appears impossible to represent.

La cabeza de Goliat centers on the process of modernization that, as we have seen, Buenos Aires had begun to experience in the twenties and thirties but which in the 1940s enters a new stage marked by the rapid development of the mass media and a marked increment in the urban population.[6] Although Argentina had had a thriving newspaper and magazine industry since the nineteenth century, in the first half of the twentieth "aparecerán otros medios que se afirman en etapas paralelas o posteriores (el cine mudo de 1900 a 1920, la radio de 1920 a 1940 y el cine sonoro de 1930 a 1945) . . . en este marco los medios argentinos se desarrollan con características propias, y en un ascenso que tiene su punto culminante en la década 1940–1950, etapa de expansión de empresas y proyectos nacionales, en radio, cine, música, revistas, etc. Ya para entonces se habían producido importantes transformaciones socio-culturales que exigen nuevas respuestas a los medios"[7] [other media establish themselves at parallel times or later (silent film from 1900 to 1920, radio from 1920 to 1940 and sound film from 1930 to 1945) . . . in this context the Argentinean media develop their own characteristics, increase and reach their peak in the decade 1940–1950, a period of development in national companies and projects in radio, film, music, journals, etc. At that time important socio-cultural changes demanded a new response to the media].

Martínez Estrada's response to the mass media is, in general,

negative.[8] The radio, Hollywood films, and popular music are com-
plicitous with the world of simulacra that for him is Buenos Aires.
Yet precisely because the media of technical reproduction, and especially photography, are so central to his analysis of the city, *La
cabeza de Goliat* serves to complicate models of homogenous identity constructions in the first half of the twentieth century by putting
into question the problem of representation.

   In his study of postnational visual culture, Nestor García Canclini
observes that in the first half of the twentieth century the mass
media in Latin America served to consolidate national identities
and to allow citizens to recognize themselves as part of a totality. It
is not until the 1970s, he argues, that this model begins to break
down with the advent of globalization and transnational production.[9] However, *La cabeza de Goliat* demonstrates that due to the
advent of the mass media in Argentina the decomposition of national identities begins much earlier. If in the nineteenth century
nation-building was synonymous with its ability to be written, as
Julio Ramos affirms, the phenomenon of technical reproducibility
will complicate this model by questioning the status of the image,
the notions of remembering and forgetting (of history) and the political uses of art (as well as the aesthetization of politics). These
problems will have profound consequences for the ways in which
the essayist thinks the concepts of collectivity and community.

   The intuitions and aporias first formulated in *La cabeza de Goliat*
regarding these questions are taken to their limits with the publication of *Muerte y Transfiguración de Martín Fierro: ensayo de interpretación de la vida argentina* [*Death and Transfiguration of
Martín Fierro: An Interpretive Essay of Argentinean Life*] in 1948.
Rejecting a hypostasized notion of community, Martínez Estrada
will posit the need for a transfiguration, a going beyond the figures
which have dominated national discourse since the Centenary:
since the inscription of a neutralizing and often violent ideology of
national cohesiveness. In *Muerte y transfiguración* Martínez Estrada will re-think the political nature of literary texts in order to
foreground their radical force. In response to the aesthetization of
politics that the works of Leopoldo Lugones and Ricardo Rojas,
among others, had produced in their different interpretations of the
poem *Martín Fierro*, Martínez Estrada will propose its re-politici-
zation. This process will entail a de-contextualization of the artwork (the poem) in order to reconfigure its function within the
country's hegemonic literary tradition.

Against an organic and totalizing notion of community, which posits a substantive identity for the collectivity (through a certain use of language, ideal place, and Subject), Martínez Estrada's texts propose the need to write in a language inscribed by the catachristic movement of translation and propose a displacement of the traditional notions of place and time, permanently distorted by the effects of the machines of reproduction. His essays thus undo static notions of origins, authenticity and history and propose a re-evaluation of the very way we read literature and literature reads community.

IMAGES OF A CITY: *La cabeza de Goliat*

The world itself has taken on a "photographic face."
—S. Kracauer, "On Photography"

Speed is what characterizes the Buenos Aires of *La cabeza de Goliat*: "La ciudad se convierte en pista de incesante tráfago, máquinas y pasajeros son arrastrados como partículas metálicas por trombas de electricidad"[10] [The city is converted into a course of incessant traffic; machines and passengers are dragged along like metallic particles, by whirlwinds of electricity]. As in his essay of 1933 the temporality of the nation in *La cabeza de Goliat* is also presented through visual metaphors, but the experience of this temporality now can only be registered by a conjunction of traces captured in the lightning speed of the photograph.

Martínez Estrada uses the photograph in order to illustrate the displacements that in the field of perception the experience of the city puts into play: "nada tiene el valor convincente de la fotografía. Convence en primer término a los ojos, que son los órganos casi exclusivos para interpretar a Buenos Aires. A Buenos Aires se lo interpreta con los ojos porque ha sido construído para ser visto. Y de ahí el poder de fascinación que ejerce" [nothing else has the convincing value of the photograph. It first convinces the eyes, which are the exclusive organs for interpreting Buenos Aires. Buenos Aires is interpreted with the eyes because it was built to be seen. There lies the power of fascination it holds] (CG 21). However, the fascinating urban perception is a form of degraded vision for Martínez Estrada and a symptom of moral decay as well:

en Buenos Aires todo está a la vista y es conocido . . . Se ve desde la
calle, sin pudor, lo que hasta entonces estaba vedado, circuido por la
intimidad de la vida doméstica. Pudor, como si se obtuviera con la violencia una desnudez. Ese empapelado, esas cornisas . . . no se hicieron
para ser vistos desde el exterior. Ahora la mirada profana los contempla
desde una distancia absurda y de manera miserable. No sólo está des-
nuda la alcoba, sino expuesta con todo lo ausente que resta en ella a la
mirada indiferente del espectador. (CG 48, 64)

[in Buenos Aires everything is in view and known . . . One can see from
the street, without shame, what until now was forbidden, enclosed in the
intimacy of domestic life. Shame, as if one could obtain nudity with
violence. That wallpaper, those cornices . . . were not made to be seen
from the outside. Now the profane gaze contemplates them from an ab-
surd distance and in a miserable way. Not only is the bedroom nude, it
is also exposed with all that is absent in it to the indifferent gaze of the
spectator.]

Martínez Estrada presents the aporias that the photograph puts
into play. On the one hand, a photographic Buenos Aires would
seem to come closer to the spectator, so much so that the spectator
even sees what he doesn't want to see—he sees too much (what
should be kept behind closed doors or even repressed)—but at the
same time the eyes with which the spectator sees the city registers
an absence ("todo lo ausente que resta en ella" [all that is absent in
it]). This aporetic relation is inherent to the photograph, given that
when something is seen with "photographic eyes," what is seen is
a reproduction and not the thing itself. As Samuel Weber notes, "to
bring something 'closer' presupposes a point or points of reference
that are sufficiently fixed, . . . self-identical, to allow for the distinction between closeness and farness, proximity and distance. Where,
however, what is 'brought closer' is itself already a reproduction—
and as such separated from itself—the closer it comes, the more
distant it is."[11]

What, if anything, can be "seen," then, of a world which, to paraphrase Kracauer, has put on a photographic face? There is a de-
contextualization at work in the photograph, a taking out of place
that does not allow for the reconstruction of a whole. The photograph is inimical to the notion of a total (and totalizing) image and
thus is able to produce only fragments.[12] The photograph thus
allows Martínez Estrada to posit that a topography of the nation is
impossible—at least a writing able to guarantee a substantive and

total apprehension of the nation. The urban, modern landscape of Buenos Aires creates modalities of perception that lead Martínez Estrada to ask if the experience of the nation does not correspond or can be better registered in a photo album than in a written text. That is, in a photographic image rather than in the space of writing:

> Cuando se nos enseñó a mirar con atención rincones y trozos insignifi-cantes de la ciudad con el ojo fotográfico—una caja de fósforos junto a la rueda de un coche, un pedazo de puerta al sol, una pierna que sube la escalera—, comprendimos que nuestros ojos están ciegos. No nos sirven nada más que como lazarillos para cruzar las calles, no tropezar con otros y ganarnos la vida. *El ojo ideal sería la célula fotoeléctrica.* La ciudad pervierte así nuestros sentidos y, finalmente, nuestra inteligen-cia, que en vez de ser órgano de percibir la belleza, el bien y la verdad, se convierte en órgano de lucha y defensa, ocupado en eludir peligros y en acrecentar las reservas de pequeñas ventajas acumulativas. Inteligen-cia en la yema de los dedos, como el ojo del ciego. (CG 84–85, my emphasis)

> [When they taught us to look attentively at the corners and insignificant fragments of the city with a photographic eye—a box of matches next to a car's tire, the frame of a door under the sun, a leg that goes up the stairs,—we understood that our eyes are blind. They are of no more use to us than as guides to cross the streets, not bump into others and earn money. *The ideal eye would be a photoelectric cell.* The city thus per-verts our senses and, finally, our intelligence, which instead of being an organ for perceiving beauty, the good and truth, is converted into a defensive and belligerent organ, occupied in eluding danger and in-creasing the reserves of small accumulated advantages. Intelligence in our fingertips, like the eye of the blind man.]

Whereas in the 1930s the writer's magisterial vision was so precise as to be able to produce an x-ray of the pampa and propose how the body of the nation could be made whole, in *La cabeza de Goliat* Martínez Estrada can only see inorganic and disarticulated frag-ments: a box of matches, a woman's leg, the frame of a door.[13] The impossibility of now using essentializing categories (beauty, good, truth) registers the change produced on the language of the nation's discourse; there is a movement away from the tropes that express the totality of the nation to others that express fragmentation and dispersal. In the photograph (in technical reproduction[14]), objects lose their "authenticity," the origin is "erased," as is its essence.

As Walter Benjamin shows in "The Work of Art in the Age of

Mechanical Reproduction," technical reproducibility is not a par-
ticularly modern phenomenon: Greek founding and stamping were
already forms of reproduction. What distinguishes reproducibility
in the middle of the twentieth century, especially in the photograph,
is how it has become a structural part of the image itself.[15] That is,
there is no "experience" of the image or the artwork that is not
already inscribed by its reproducibility. This fact has a profound
effect not only on cognitive capacity, as we saw earlier, but also on
the questions of origins, of memory and the very idea of history. It
is this last problematic that Martínez Estrada has in mind when he
likens Buenos Aires to a photographic image: "Buenos Aires ha
avanzado borrando sus pasos . . . borrar las huellas se convierte en:
iniciar una vida nueva, una nueva historia, una nueva aventura. . . .
Los demoledores borran su propio pasado, arrasando con el
Pasado . . ." [Buenos Aires has advanced erasing its steps . . . to
erase footprints means: to begin a new life, a new history, a new
adventure. . . . Those who demolish, erase their own past, sweeping
away the Past] (CG 61–63).

Martínez Estrada clearly bemoans the loss of a notion of history
as continuous and homogenous; that "new" history which the photographic image puts into play cannot reconstitute the Past; there
can be no mimetic representation of it, but at the same time the
newness which the present reveals cannot itself be made present.
Rather, it is continually disappearing, much like the image in a photograph: "cada día recomienza en el lugar que cesó la noche anterior, y es como si girara sobre sí mismo por una fuerza que nace de
su interior, busca irradiarse y no lo consigue" [every day begins
again where it left off the night before, and it is as if it revolved
around itself by a force that rose from its inside, sought to irradiate
itself, but was unable to do so] (CG 23). The impossibility of an
"irradiating" center, one capable of allowing a re-presentation of
the past, gives way to a differential relation in time that precludes
continuity. As Eduardo Cadava shows, the photograph as the "medium of likeness, speaks only of what is unlike" and history becomes an impossible memory, a forgetting.[16]

WRITING/SPEAKING NATION

The constant movement and fluidity which now marks the temporality of the city gives way to a different notion of time than that

which has traditionally dominated the essay of national identity. In this genre, horizontality and homogenization have predominated. These characteristics are condensed in a historicist narrative which does not admit fissures and where the People always appear as a unity and as a community. As Homi Bhabha has described it, the historicist narrative is pedagogical and "founds its authority in a tradition of the people . . . encapsulated in a succession of historical moments that represents an eternity produced by self-generation."[17]

If the truth of a nation's pedagogical discourse is founded on historical continuity, on a realist narrative dependent on the notion of an authentic origin and unending progress, then *La cabeza de Goliat* speaks of the impossibility of producing that type of discourse. However, the essay does not simply respond to that impossibility by positing a simple inversion or even an oppositional relation with the homogeneous national discourses of the past; it does not propose a fragmentary, disjointed, inorganic national discourse in opposition to a homogeneous one. Rather, *La cabeza de Goliat* shows how the modes of technical reproduction described in the essay present the limits of concepts such as time, narrative, image, etc. and thus serve to undermine their homogenous, unifying, and continuous presence in the so-called national discourse.

The function of photography in *La cabeza de Goliat* "illustrates" the differential relation to which we are referring. Even though the goal of the essayist is a representation which will produce an organic image of itself (the telos of the essay of national "being" ["el ser nacional"]), in the essay that image is itself unrepresentable. The heterogeneous structure of the essay presents the problem of this double movement. *La cabeza de Goliat* consists of a series of *tableaux vivants*: short sketches of urban life that include unusual characters, typical or eccentric scenes, and descriptions of customs and celebrations. The essay also has short chapters made up of dialogues, anecdotes, architectural descriptions and memories.[18] The text, then, is itself the effect of the blindness of that urban photographer's eye which Martínez Estrada criticized, the only "organ" now capable of capturing the inorganic traces and fragments of urban life.

If *Radiografía* functioned as a prescription of how Argentineans could live as a community "unidos en salud" [united in health], the Buenos Aires of 1940 puts that realization in doubt. *La cabeza de Goliat* is faced with the challenge of again offering criteria for resolving the question of national unity, a question which is not only key for the concept of nation, but also for the poetic project of the essayist of national identity, given that the photographic Buenos Aires he describes threatens to eliminate his very function. That is, if the nation can no longer be defined as an apprehensible totality, if the notion of unity, no matter how heterogeneous, is dissolved, then so are the terms of the exposition.

In his study of the notion of authority in Latin American literature, Roberto González Echevarría demonstrates how the essay depends on the representation of "the self of the author, bearing his or her public name [who] puts on a performance in which the possibility of persuasion depends on the role he/she assumes and on the fictional enclosure within which the performance takes place . . . the elaboration of a relationship between the stated intentions of the self in pursuit of presence and truth and of the fiction created to carry out that pursuit is the main figural activity that allows the performance to take place."[19] The figure of the author in González Echevarría's study is thus associated with power and persuasion, but also with violence and a dictatorial stance. The author is the very figure of knowledge and truth, the possessor and transmitter of the tradition: the voice of the community.

This type of authorial voice can be found in Martínez Estrada's *Radiografía de la pampa*. The hermeneutics of the 1933 essay allow the essayist to present the hidden wrongs ("los males") that affect a not yet realized national identity and unity. Martínez Estrada repeatedly uses the paradoxical statement in order to structure his argument, since this rhetorical device allows him to emit a statement that may seem false but proves to be true upon inspection.[20] The paradox thus allows him to be the prime interpreter, an authority that both tells the nation's hidden story and provides the cure for its self-realization.

The question of authority is also developed in *Radiografía* through its connection with European knowledge. In *Radiografía*, authority (rationality, history) is located in Europe and its knowledge is a source to which Argentina can only accede mimetically. During the 1930s, the visitors (Waldo Frank, Count Keyserling, and José Ortega y Gasset, for example) who arrived in Argentina in order to discover "lo americano" were celebrated and admired and it was their gazes that were privileged. *Radiografía* clearly echoes this sentiment. However, in *La cabeza de Goliat* Europe is no longer considered to be the foundation of truth and the visitors who now arrive to deliver conferences are an object of suspicion and even of ridicule:

> Es un lujo y un espectáculo, el conferenciante. Se lo trae desde lejanas tierras a que nos diga lo que sabemos o lo que no nos importaba, antes de su llegada; saber sin que nos importe lo que dicen ni lo que escriben. ¿Saben ellos por qué se los llama? Exóticos personajes para mirar y admirar, como las fieras del zoológico. Es el acto de la comedia intelectual mejor acogido, que ellos saben que están representando y que nosotros sabemos que tenemos que aplaudir. ¿Creen que vienen para ser escuchados y aprovechar de sus conocimientos? Se los trae para contemplarlos y para adornar la ciudad, como a un cuadro para adornar la sala. (136)[21]

> [The lecturer is a luxury and a spectacle. He is brought from afar so that he may tell us what we know or did not care about before his arrival; to know without caring what they say or write. Do they know why they are invited? Exotic characters to look at and admire like the beasts at the zoo. It is a well-accepted act of intellectual comedy, which they know they are representing and we know we have to applaud. Do they believe that they come to be heard and for us to take advantage of their knowledge? They are brought in order to look at them and adorn the city, like a picture to adorn a room.]

In *La cabeza de Goliat* Martínez Estrada notes the difference between the situation of the travelers of the past and the visitors of the present, especially in relation to the urban experience he describes in the essay:

> Desde aquellos viajeros ingleses que poco después de la Independencia iniciaron el crucero a estas tierras en busca de minas y de curiosidades, casi ha sido ininterrumpida la visita de los huéspedes que se han creído en el deber de retribuir en la forma para ellos más adecuada los halagos de la hospitalidad. Con la diferencia de que aquellos viajeros inaugurales eran incomparablemente más caballeros, perspicaces y comprensivos. Además, escribían mejor . . . En general, estimaban a nuestro país en sus características y peculiaridades penetrando en el sentido de las cosas mejor que los nativos. Los huéspedes recientes y los comensales ya encontraron una ciudad de fisonomía muy compleja para poder interpretarla, ni siquiera comprenderla. (135)

> [Ever since those English travelers that after Independence began crossing to these shores in search of mines and curiosities, the visits of those guests that have felt the need to repay our hospitality has been almost

uninterrupted. Except that those first travelers were gentlemen, more perspicacious and understanding. Furthermore, they wrote better . . . In general, they valued our country for its characteristics and peculiarities, penetrating in the meaning of things better than the natives did. The more recent visitors and guests find a city with a physiognomy too complex to interpret, much less to understand.]

The distance that separates the epistemological presuppositions of *Radiografía* from those of *La cabeza de Goliat* is demonstrated in the role that "seeing" holds in both essays. As we have shown, in *Radiografía* the eye is privileged: as the guardian of a transcendental and atemporal gaze, the essayist/radiographer and the foreign visitors are the sources of knowledge and truth. They are discoverers, seekers, and makers of meaning. However, in *La cabeza de Goliat*, Martínez Estrada realizes that the gaze is no longer privileged and contains no essential knowledge. What truth can be discovered, what knowledge transmitted when the gaze is now that of a "célula fotoeléctrica" [photoelectric cell] and the image that is produced is the fragmented and ghostly imprint of a photograph? The self who writes, if one can still speak of a self in the context of this essay, is now the impoverished eye of the blind man.

As González Echevarría shows, the master/teacher's voice in *Ariel* resonates violently, much like the machines that Rodó condemns as inimical to the transmission of the nation's spirit. Rodó's authoritative and authoritarian stance is far from the degraded and defensive mechanical eye described by Martínez Estrada. Indeed, in the passage from *Radiografía* to *La cabeza de Goliat*, one could read the beginning of the end of that tradition of the magisterial essay of national identity whose origin González Echevarría locates in Rodó's *Ariel*.

In his essay of 1940 Martínez Estrada affirms that Buenos Aires can no longer be a metonym for the Nation (as in Sarmiento's paradigmatic case) given that the signifier "Buenos Aires" erodes all substantive certainties. If for Sarmiento Buenos Aires was to function as the center of a national unity so desired and methodically planned, *La cabeza de Goliat* offers its decapitated head, the fragments of a now impossible political project.

The difficulties in imagining the outlines of national identity and unity become even more pronounced in *Sarmiento* (1946), the first of three studies Martínez Estrada dedicates to the author of *Facundo*.[22] This text is directly linked to the context of European fascism, as well as to the effects of what Martínez Estrada views as the fascist phenomenon in Argentina: Peronism, which rose to power in 1946. Martínez Estrada's ideas on fascism and Peronism are in line with those of *Sur*, the literary magazine he joined in 1946. The magazine's position is summed up by María Rosa Oliver: "El fascismo, para nosotros . . . se encarnaba en Perón, sus epígonos los nacionalistas (con o sin uniforme) y el clero que hasta los confesionarios lo apoyaba" [Fascism, for us, was incarnated in Peron, his disciples, the nationalists (with or without uniform), and the clergy, who even supported him in the confessionals.][23]

Martínez Estrada reads the fascist phenomenon as a direct consequence of Sarmiento's legacy, both in its thirst for capitalist expansion and in its homogenizing nationalist ideology. In *Sarmiento*, the adoption of "civilized" forms results in that dialectic of the enlightenment that T. Adorno and M. Horkheimer locate in the homology between progress and domination:[24]

De ellos se aproprió brutalmente Hitler, precipitándose a consumarlos por métodos de conquista por las armas, para cuya osadía contaba con esas fuerzas de la barbarie que Sarmiento vio aflorar en suelo americano, pero que constituía el subsuelo de la misma civilización capitalista. La política internacional inglesa y americana de postguerra, como la hitlerista que la procedió con más franca brutalidad, plantea la cuestión de qué significa uno o varios tipos de naciones civilizadas. Para Sarmiento civilización era todo aquello que había hecho de Inglaterra y de Estados Unidos naciones poderosas, industrialmente desarrolladas, comercial y socialmente organizadas, económica y culturalmente eficaces; pero no se había preguntado qué diferencias y concordancias hay entre la barbarie de los pueblos primitivos y la civilización de los pueblos decadentes. La grandeza que Sarmiento anhela es precisamente la grandeza que encubre la injusticia, la crueldad, la infamia, la codicia . . . Sin un plan social de justicia, el progreso es una maldición.[25]

[Hitler appropriated them brutally, consummating them with armed conquest, for whose boldness he counted with the barbaric forces Sarmiento saw flourish on American soil, but which constituted the ground of capitalist civilization. Post-war English and American international politics, like Hitler's that preceded them with more brutality, poses the question of what one or various types of civilized nations signify. For Sarmiento civilization was everything that had made England and the United States powerful nations, industrially developed, commercially and socially organized, economically and culturally efficient, but he did not ask himself what differences and similarities there are between the barbarism of primitive peoples and the civilization of decadent ones. The greatness Sarmiento desires is precisely that greatness that conceals injustice, cruelty, infamy and greed . . . Without a social plan of justice, progress is a curse.]

The Enlightenment philosophy that informed Sarmiento's political projects had as its goal to liberate human beings from prejudice and superstition and to declare his sovereignty as thinking and rational being. But for Martínez Estrada fascism (and capitalism) shows that those same ideals can result in the exploitation of prejudice and ignorance. Instead of sovereignty, totalitarianism; instead of liberating progress, the use of instrumental reason at the service of the will to power. It is the necessary violence that fascism inscribes within the community that Martínez Estrada denounces.

The fascist phenomenon evinces, for Martínez Estrada, the permanent tension between the presuppositions of Enlightenment philosophy and those of the *Volkgeist*:[26]

Un ciudadano es ya un conflicto histórico y en sí mismo lidian dos ejércitos. Usa los artefactos de una técnica del orden internacional, aprende su manejo, se instruye en ciencias y en especialidades que requieren una visión total del mundo correspondiente a otros horizontes, y sin embargo permanece fiel a normas de existencia y de pensamiento que corresponden a otras formas locales de humanidad. Es internacionalista y nacionalista cabalmente al revés. (*Sarmiento* 86)

[A citizen is a historical conflict in whom two armies are at war. He uses the artifacts of the technology of the international order, he learns their implementation, he educates himself in sciences and specialties that require a total vision of the world which correspond to other horizons, but he remains faithful to norms of existence and thought which correspond to other local forms of humanity. He is internationalist and nationalist in perfectly reverse order.]

Martínez Estrada's observations on fascism point to the aporia of the modern nation. As we noted in the introduction, the concept of nation and of national subject (citizen) requires a future-oriented, progressive teleology, as well as a pre-modern appeal to blood and soil. In other words, the national subject embodies a universal logic that is nevertheless anchored in a timeless, particular essence. For Martínez Estrada this contradiction will result in a displacement of the concept of nation, a necessary strategy in order for the essay to reconfigure the contemporary functions of literature and culture

If in the citizen two armies are at war, to which nation does he belong, what is his nationality? In *Sarmiemto* Martínez Estrada claims that fascism makes nationalism and totalitarianism equivalent terms and, for this reason, he legitimizes the rights of the noncitizen. Ironically, that is also Sarmiento's "tragedy": Martínez Estrada considers that Sarmiento could understand Argentina only when he was in exile. In *Muerte y transfiguración de Martín Fierro*, the notion of the non-citizen and of exile will be further developed as forms of avoiding the aesthetization of politics which, as Walter Benjamin has shown, is at the heart of the fascist ideology.

The Ends of Myth: Muerte y transfiguración de *Martín Fierro*

The technology of reproduction, one might say generally, detaches the reproduced object from the domain of tradition.
—Walter Benjamin, "The Work of Art in the Age of Mechanical Reproduction"

The repeated and erroneous readings that the poem *Martín Fierro* has endured since its publication in 1872, its various deaths, as Martínez Estrada puts it, were the motivation behind his 1948 essay titled *Muerte y transfiguración de Martín Fierro: ensayo de interpretación de la vida argentina*. Since the 1910s, the centenary of Argentina's independence, the poem had been read as the bedrock of Argentina's literary tradition.[27] Both the modernist poet Leopoldo Lugones and the writer Ricardo Rojas proclaim the epic quality of *Martín Fierro*: for Rojas, "la obra de Hernández representaba para los argentinos lo que la *Chanson de Roland* para los franceses y el *Mio Cid* para los españoles" [Hernández's work represented for Argentineans what the *Chanson de Roland* was for the French and the *Mio Cid* for the Spanish] and for Lugones, *Martín Fierro* is likened to the Homeric poems that "formaron el núcleo de la nacionalidad helénica" [formed the nucleus of Hellenic nationality].[28] Because of its "transhistoric presence," it is also the conscience of the nation, the "epic of democracy," Rojas claims, and thus the basis of national identity and national unity.[29]

Lugones's and Rojas's interpretations of *Martín Fierro* aestheticize the political content of the work by positing the organic unity of the nation embodied in the poem. As Phillipe Lacoue-Labarthe notes regarding the fascist notion of art, the *Gesamtkunstwerk* [the total art work] not only "offers the truth of the polis or the State, but . . . the political itself is instituted and constituted (and regularly regrounds itself) in and as a work of art."[30] Indeed, in his first lectures on *Martín Fierro*, Lugones implores his listeners to study the poem because "así se cumple con la civilización y con la patria . . . estudiando la tradición de la raza, no para incrustarse en ella, sino para descubrir la ley del progreso que nos revelará el ejercicio eficaz de la vida, en estados paulatinamente superiores"[31] [In this way one does one's duty with civilization and with the nation . . . studying the race's tradition, not in order to embed oneself in it, but in order to discover the law of progress that will reveal to us the efficacious practice of life, in progressively superior states] and "Felicítome por haber sido el agente de una íntima comunicación nacional entre la poesía del pueblo y la mente culta de la clase superior; que así es como se forma el espíritu de la patria" [I congratulate myself for being the agent of an intimate national communication between the poetry of the people and the cultured minds of the upper class, which is how the spirit of the nation is formed] (P 201). For Lugones the poem is where the nation finds itself reflected ("esta unanimidad nacional así revelada") [that national unanimity so revealed] P 200), where it can identify itself, assume a body and a voice: where the nation can be represented.[32]

Muerte y transfiguración is a direct attack on Lugones and the aesthetic project he proposes in *El payador* (1916):

> *El payador*, que no se refiere sino incidentalmente al Poema, . . . es el cuño en que se funde la nueva efigie de aquel patriotismo de destierro que campea después en toda obra de rehabilitación del Poema. Desde ese momento el poema queda convertido en cantera de nacionalidad, y los críticos ulteriores se encaminan en esos yacimientos, mejor que al texto, para cohonestar una concepción épica de la historia que, de la Independencia acá, no tiene otro héroe a que acudir sino ese pobre cantor y peleador que en lugar de ser un héroe, sólo viene a representar un papel heroico de la gesta.[33]

> [*El payador*, which refers to the poem only in passing, . . . is the stamp in which the new image of that exiled patriotism is cast and later abounds in all rehabilitative works of the poem. From that moment on the poem is converted into a repository of nationality and later critics head toward those deposits instead of toward the text, in order to gloss

over an epic version of history which, since Independence, has no other hero than that poor fighter and singer that, instead of being a hero, only represents a heroic role in the exploits.]

If, for Lugones, the poem represents the nation's final break with Spain, thus serving as a symbol of an autonomous national identity, Martínez Estrada affirms that Spain does not produce, after the 18th century, anything as Spanish as the poem.[34] In order to wrest *Martín Fierro* from its inaugural role, he dates it as prior to the nation. In fact, for Martínez Estrada, Hernández reinstates the colonial period in the very language he uses: "Rosas instaura la Colonia en los mecanismos de la vida pública y en las costumbres, Hérnandez [la instaura] en el idioma" [Rosas establishes the Colony in the mechanisms of public life and in customs; Hernández establishes it in the language] (MT 293). The poem thus becomes a denunciation against those who founded the nation. Through this strategic analogy, Martínez Estrada equates Lugones's and Rojas's reading of the poem with the political and cultural programs of the "founding fathers." Just as the governments of "order and progress" (the political emblem of liberalism) killed the gaucho, the readings that Rojas and Lugones institutionalized marked the end of gauchesca literature: "con el *Martín Fierro*, la literatura gauchesca termina. Era un principio y sin embargo fue un fin" [with *Martín Fierro* gauchesque literature ends. It was supposed to be a beginning, yet it was an end] (MT 294).

To counter Rojas's and Lugones's nationalistic claims, Martínez Estrada affirms, "Pero en el poema ese sentimiento [de patriotismo] no existe en absoluto . . . Ninguno de los personajes tiene conciencia del país en que ha nacido como unidad espiritual, Nación, estado o raza" [But in the poem that feeling [of patriotism] does not exist at all . . . None of the characters is conscious of the country in which he was born as spiritual unit, Nation, State, or Race] (MT 370). In Martínez Estrada's reading of the poem *Martín Fierro* is pre-national, unpatriotic and thus unable to represent the unity and cohesiveness of the nation. Martínez Estrada's dispute with the cultural nationalism of Lugones and Rojas centers on the term that has characterized the debate on these issues: "el ser nacional." This term can be translated into English as a national being or national subject and presupposes the nation as subject, as the common ground on which the logic of the community is founded. This logic, dependent on a notion of a fixed place, surrounded by borders and frontiers, is also the basis of all nationalist as well as totalitarian ideologies.

In order to problematize the contiguity between nation and being, or to unground the notion of community, Martínez Estrada deterritorializes the poem *Martín Fierro* and many other texts which have been traditionally considered to constitute Argentina's literary tradition:

> Sin una lectura de fondo; sin por lo menos centenares de obras escritas y profusamente leídas con el mismo propósito de explorar nuestra realidad, *el Santos Vega* de Ascasubi, el *Facundo*, el *Martín Fierro*, el *Matadero, Amalia*, muchas obras de Hudson y los informes de los viajeros ingleses . . . no pasan de ser cuerpos extraños en el organismo de nuestra literatura. Pero estas obras están desterradas, fuera del juego, y el sentido vivo de nuestra realidad es una visión propia del desterrado. (MT 308)

> [Without a profound interpretation, without at least hundreds of works written and profusely read with the same goal of exploring our reality, *Santos Vega* by *Ascasubi, Facundo, Martín Fierro, El Matadero, Amalia*, many works by Hudson and the reports of the English travelers . . . are nothing more than foreign bodies in the organism of our literature. But these works are exiled, out of play and the living sense of our reality is the vision of the exile.]

Martínez Estrada enacts an innovative reading of Argentinean literature here: he places the texts by the nineteenth-century founders of Argentina's literary tradition alongside others by the Anglo-Argentinean William Henry Hudson and the English travel writers: texts first written in another language. The battle cry of cultural nationalism had been "One people/One language" that, much as for the Romantics, presupposed the unity and homogeneity of the national language, unsullied by the contamination of others. As we saw earlier, this tradition is still evident in Lugones's lectures on the *Martín Fierro*, where he contrasts the pristine language of Hernandez's poem (emblematic of national identity) to that of the Italian and Spanish immigrants then arriving in Argentina: "es una verdad histórica que los poemas homéricos formaron el núcleo de la nacionalidad helénica. Saber decirlos bien era el rasgo característico del griego. Bárbaro significaba revesado, tartamudo: nuestro gringo" [it is a historical truth that the Homeric poems formed the nucleus of Hellenic nationality. To recite them well was characteris-

tic of the Greek. Barbarian meant unruly, a stutterer: our *gringo*]
(50–51).

To counter Lugones's interpretation, Martínez Estrada emphasizes the decentered speech of gauchesque literature, of the exiled
Sarmiento, of the Anglo-Argentinean William Henry Hudson and
of the English travelers to the River Plate region: the language of
translation, never totally national, never completely foreign. Martínez Estrada's reading depends on the belief that the language of
translation is proper not only to texts that are outside the nation's
literary tradition but also to those which are considered to be the
very foundation of that tradition. Tradition and national literature
thus become divorced from the very ground that is supposed to sustain them, thus giving way to an idea of literature not bound by a
notion of place (of geography, of language). If the contiguity between nation and being ("ser nacional") is no longer sustainable,
then Martínez Estrada's reading of literary tradition allows for a
notion of a literature which is Argentinean, but no longer national.

THE NATION IN TRANSLATION: ON WILLIAM HENRY HUDSON

> los ingleses—algunos—, los trashumantes y andariegos, ejercen
> una facultá de empaparse en forasteras variaciones del ser: un
> desinglesamiento despacito, instintivo, que los americaniza, los
> asiatiza, los africaniza, y los salva.

> [the English—some of them—, the nomadic and wandering
> ones, have the ability to steep themselves in alien variations of
> being: a slow and instinctive de-Englishing that Americanizes
> them, Asiatizes them, Africanizes them and saves them].
> —Jorge Luis Borges, "La tierra cárdena" (1926) ["The Purple Land"]

As elsewhere throughout their careers, there are points of contact
between Martínez Estrada's ideas on the impossibility of an "authentic" national language and those that Jorge Luis Borges expressed in a review of the Anglo-Argentinean writer William Henry
Hudson. Advocating a displacement of the borders that traditionally
constitute a national language, Borges writes: "Percibir o no los
matices criollos es quizá baladí, pero el hecho es que de todos los
extranjeros . . . nadie los percibe sino el inglés"[35] [To perceive the
criollo (creole) nuances is perhaps trivial, but the fact is that of all
the foreigners . . . no one perceives them but the English]. The term

criollo here functions as a synecdoche for what is authentically Argentinean, but it is an uncanny *criollismo*. While Lugones locates foreignness (the immigrants) as exterior to the unity or wholeness of Argentinean language, for Borges what is considered one's own and proper language can best (can only?) be expressed by/in a foreign tongue. The Argentinean language is itself a foreign language, Borges seems to indicate.

It is important to note that Borges maintains the ambiguity of the name at the end of the quote ("nadie los percibe sino el inglés," he states) given that "inglés" can refer both to the language and to the nationality. Of course, it is precisely the impossibility of fixing a stable, unambiguous meaning on to the signifier that it at stake here; that is, of making language and nationality homologous. Borges maintains the ambiguity of the name intact in order to undermine that homology.

Martínez Estrada also notes the uncanny unhomeliness of Hudson's prose:

una inquietante extranjería en su idioma inglés bien castizo. Se ha dicho, para explicarlo, que Hudson pensaba en castellano y traducía al escribir; pero esto no puede ser cierto, desde que con los años el idioma que aprendió de chico . . . se fue borrando por falta de ejercicio, hasta hacérsele penoso hablarlo. Y esto precisamente cuando al final de su vida sintió como una necesidad . . . el hablar castellano. Verdad es que aunque hablara durante treinta y tantos años este idioma, más familiar le era el inglés, y que necesitó formarse una lengua literaria mediante un estudio de este idioma parecido al que realizó Conrad. Aquello de extraño que hallaba el lector insular en la prosa de Hudson es precisamente lo que hallamos de nuestro en las traducciones: el espíritu de nuestro país tal como se refleja en la lengua que hablamos.[36]

[a disturbing foreignness in his Castillian English. In order to explain it, it has been said that Hudson thought in Spanish and translated as he wrote, but this cannot be true, since with the passing of time the language he learned as a child began to fade for wont of use, until it became difficult to speak it. And this occurred precisely at the end of his life, when he felt the need to speak . . . Spanish. It is true that although he spoke this language for thirty some years, English was more familiar to him, and it was necessary for him to create a literary language by way of English, much as Conrad did. What the English reader found strange in Hudson's prose is precisely what we feel is most ours in the translations: the spirit of our country as it is reflected in the language we speak.]

Hudson's prose displays the linguistic difference inscribed in language itself; the coexistence of several languages within a single tongue—language's very impurity. Translation, understood as what maintains the multiplicity of language intact, becomes the model for an "Argentinean literature." In fact, for Martínez Estrada, Hudson's texts accomplish what he believes the Argentinean writer, tied to the forms of a cultured Spanish, to what he calls "ready made forms," is unable to produce.[37]

Octavio Paz's study of the translation process proves useful in understanding why Martínez Estrada privileges Hudson's written language. Paz focuses on translation's relation to key rhetorical figures:

> todas las traducciones son operaciones que se sirven de los dos modos de expresión a que, según Roman Jakobson, se reducen todos los procedimientos literarios: la metonimia y la metáfora. El texto original jamás reaparece (sería imposible) en la otra lengua; no obstante, está presente siempre porque en la traducción, sin decirlo, lo menciona constantemente o lo convierte en un objeto verbal que, aunque distinto, lo reproduce: metonimia o metáfora. Las dos, a diferencia de las traducciones explicativas y de la paráfrasis, son formas rigurosas y que no están reñidas con la exactitud: la primera es una descripción indirecta y la segunda una ecuación verbal.[38]

> [all translations are operations served by the two modes of expression to which, according to Roman Jakobson, all literary processes are reduced: metonymy and metaphor. The original text never re-appears in the other language (that would be impossible); however, it is present because the translation mentions it constantly, without saying so, or converts it into a verbal object which, although different, reproduces it: metonymy or metaphor. Contrary to explicatory translations or those based on paraphrases, both metonymy and metaphor are rigorous forms and not at odds with exactness: the former is an indirect description and the latter a verbal equation.]

Although he rejects the notion of a translation's literal reproduction of the original text, Paz does propose a traditional definition of metaphor and metonymy as tropes capable of presenting a resemblance (metaphor) or a correspondence (metonymy). In both cases, there is a transfer of sense and a movement toward the recuperation, although imperfect or inexact, of the original. The *Oxford English Dictionary* defines interpretation as the act of expounding meaning,

but also as the act of translation; it is this equivalence that Paz keeps
intact in his definition of translation.

Walter Benjamin's theory of translation differs markedly from
Paz's: "If the kinship of languages manifests itself in translations,
this is not accomplished through a vague alikeness between adapta-
tion and original. It stands to reason that kinship does not necessarily involve likeness . . . it cannot be defined adequately by identity
of origin."[39] Translation cannot be thought within the genealogical
line of heredity and resemblance. Indeed, the word *aufgabe* in Benjamin's essay points to this impossibility. This word can be translated as task, duty, but also as defeat, a giving up or surrender.
What translations make evident is the fissure in what is considered
to be the original, mother tongue. Far from being familiar, safe and
proper, translation reveals the "foreignness" in our own language.[40]

What is the relation, then, between translation and "original"?
Translation and original become fragments of a "greater language,"
as Benjamin states, which is at the same time the impetus for translation (the dream of transparent communicability) and the greatest
of impossibilities (the multiplicity of tongues prevents the dream
becoming a reality). The relation between translation and original
can thus only be (as Benjamin calls it) "an infinitely small point,"
a place which is in fact a non-place as it precludes unity or convergence.

Martínez Estrada will name this point "catachresis":

Se establece una tensión permanente, una presión deformadora, en
quien usa de una lengua para expresar sentimientos e ideas que respon-
den a una información o cultura cuyo órgano de expresión es otra lengua . . . La palabra sufre así una violencia interior, no en su morfología
sino en su sentido, y es el fenómeno universal y extrañísimo de la meta
morfosis semántica, en el caso lingüístico denominado catácresis. (MT
235)

[A permanent tension, a deforming pressure is established in someone
who uses one language in order to express feelings and ideas that respond to information or a culture whose means of expression is another
language . . . The word thus suffers an interior violence, not in its mor-
phology, but in its meaning, and it is the universal and strange phenomenon of semantic metamorphosis in the linguistic case called
catachresis.]

Martínez Estrada also values this linguistic violence in Franz Kafka: "Este ser alienus, de otra raza, de otra configuración psíquica y onírica . . . fue el judío checo que escribió en alemán y pensó en hebreo: F. Kafka"[41] [This alien being, from another race, from another psychic and oneiric configuration . . . was the Czech Jew who wrote in German and thought in Hebrew: F. Kafka]. Kafka, "a stranger in his own land," is able to work the German language from "within" as if it were itself a foreign language and thus enact those differential traits that are properly catachrestic.

Catachresis is defined as the misapplication of a word from its normal or proper significance. Because of its unique and strange configuration, critics have noted that catachresis is both outside and inside the tropological system, given that it is a figurative use of language and yet also a proper or literal name for something: "to give a 'face' to a mountain or a 'head' to a cabbage or lettuce is clearly a figure [but since it] does not take the place of an already existent, established use but rather replaces the lack of the literal, the lack of the proper expression, it is not just figurative; it can often become the proper, the only way to say the X of a mountain."[42] As a model for translation, catachresis has an ambiguous position. Since it functions as a proper name and as a common noun, it both requires translation and makes translation impossible.

With catachresis as his model, the task of the translator no longer becomes one of restituting in the translation what was first given in the original—a task that is altogether impossible to accomplish and must inevitably lead to defeat. Catachresis implies a lack in the original, not something that was given and lost but something it never had to begin with. In "The Task of the Translator," Benjamin quotes Mallarmé on this point: "The imperfection of languages consists in their plurality, the supreme one is lacking . . . the diversity of idioms on earth prevents everyone from uttering the words which would otherwise, at one single stroke . . . materialize as truth."[43] The original is already incomplete, in the place of a lack, in a permanent exile, But, of course, exile also become a doubtful concept, given that there is no longer a home or a home(land) from which to be exiled.

Catachrestic writing thus puts in doubt the notion of the quest of identity as an intrinsic part of Latin American texts. As we saw in the introduction, even if the quest is marked by divagation or wandering that seems to put in doubt the coherent circularity of the process, the economy of travel forms the basis of the quests of identity and thus requires a place (the home) to function as a point of reference, the absolute beginning and end of meaning. Catachrestic writing no longer allows for this model to function. Catachresis, as a figure, is a mere marker, a placeholder; it has nothing to do with sense, in the double meaning of the word, as meaning and as direction. Catachresis thus names a writing which does not function as a dwelling place for identity since, as we saw above, it puts in doubt the very possibility of representation.

Translation as a spatial relation is also complicated in catachresis. As a placeholder or marker, catachresis not only does away with the notion of homeland, but also with the notion of a fixed ground or space. Whereas traditional notions of translation imply a transference (from one place to another: original to translation); catachrestic translations (place as non-place) function much like G. Deleuze and F. Guattari's notion of nomadism, where the points traveled are indefinite and non-communicating:

> The nomad is not at all the same as the migrant; for the migrant goes principally from one point to another, even if the second point is uncertain, unforeseen, or not well localized . . . nomads have no points, paths, or lands, even though they do so by all appearances. If the nomad can be called the Deterritorialized par excellence, it is precisely because there is no reterritorialization afterward as with the migrant.[44]

The distinction between the migrant and the nomad is an important one. While the migrant still adheres to a notion of home (one that is perhaps hostile and unlivable), the nomad can never be said to depart because there is no home to leave or go to. Nomadism further complicates the notion of transference as movement (from one point to another) given that the nomad is "he who does not move"; borders, frontiers, or enclosures do not delimit the space he inhabits.[45] The nomad is thus a placeholder, a marker that cannot be fixed, located, or identified. The nomad assumes the catachrestic figure of translation.

How would (and/or could) a nomadic literature be written, and what are the effects of a language that is catachrestic? Martínez Estrada's texts lead to an inevitable question: can the nation still be narrated? Once the various forms of interruption are shown to be at work within a text, after the coherence and integrity of concepts such as language, image, origins, authenticity, history have been taken to their limit and read as the limit which precludes all possibility of representation, can a narration still be produced? For critics such as Homi Bhabha the answer is yes, as the title to his well-known book of essays *Nation and Narration* attests: the performative discourse of the minority can interrupt (though not eliminate) the pedagogical discourse of the nation and produce its own counter-narrative.

However, does a simple inversion of the tropes that have dominated pedagogical discourse suffice to sustain such a narration? As we saw in the introduction, there are dangers in producing oppositional discourses or narrations, while still maintaining or re-inscribing the conceptual framework that they seek to dismantle. Although the texts by Martínez Estrada studied in this chapter present alternatives for thinking or even making impossible a national narrative based on homogenizing definitions of concepts such as language, literature and culture, they do not provide an answer to narration's "beyond." As we will see in Paz, and especially in our study of Borges, the question of writing will be crucial for presenting alternative forms of community not tied to traditional paradigms of narration.

3
On Being Mexican, for Example: Octavio Paz and the Dialectics of Universality

La conversión de la sociedad en comunidad y la del poema en poesía práctica no están a la vista. Lo contrario es lo cierto: cada día aparecen más lejanas.

[The conversion of society into community and the poem into practical poetry are not within view. It is just the opposite: each day they seem more remote.]
—O. Paz, *El arco y la lira* [*The Bow and the Lyre*]

nos buscábamos a nosotros mismos
y encontramos a los otros.

[we were looking for ourselves and found others.]
—O. Paz, "Entrada retrospectiva" [Retrospective Approach]

POETRY AND COMMUNITY ARE AT ONCE THE CENTRAL PROBLEMATICS in many of Octavio Paz's texts as well as an always-receding horizon irreducible to place, politics, or poetics. *El laberinto de la soledad* [*The Labyrinth of Solitude*] (1950), which ostensibly is concerned with the particularity of the Mexican man and woman (his/her identity) and *El arco y la lira* [*The Bow and the Lyre*] (1956), which proposes a definition of the poetic act, show the aporias at work in the attempt to circumscribe and delimit what the texts propose to identify. In these texts of the 1950s Paz confronts the problematic relations between the commonality of human existence and the singularity of being human, the play between the concepts of particularity and universality, as well as writing (poetry) and modernity.[1] Throughout his texts Paz attempts to respond to a question he first articulates in *El laberinto de la soledad*: "¿cómo crear una sociedad, una cultura, que no niegue nuestra humanidad

74

pero tampoco la convierta en una vana abstracción?" [how should a society and a culture that do not negate our humanity or covert it into a vain abstraction be created?].[2] That is, how can community be thought outside the parameters that have conventionally defined the quest of identity without erasing or neutralizing the singularity of being Mexican?

Paz explains the inter-relatedness of these two texts in an interview now published as "En el filo del viento: México y Japón." Paz states: "El tema de la poesía me llevó a escribir muchos ensayos y dos libros . . . Pero otro tema—otro misterio—me interesó tanto o más: qué significa ser mexicano? Esta pregunta sobre México y sobre los mexicanos es también una pregunta sobre mí mismo. Y así surgieron mis dos primeros libros de ensayos: *El laberinto de la soledad* y *El arco y la lira*: dos respuestas a dos preguntas. Todo lo que he escrito después ha sido, en cierto modo, el desarrollo de estos dos libros."[3] [The topic of poetry led me to write many essays and two books . . . But another topic—another mystery—intrigued me equally or more: what does being Mexican mean? This question about Mexico and about the Mexicans is also a question about myself. My first two books of essays, *The Labyrinth of Solitude* and *The Bow and the Lyre*, emerged in this way: two answers to two questions. Everything I've written subsequently has been, in a certain way, the development of those two books]. The texts' relatedness becomes itself an exploration of the question of relation, of the ways in which the literary (the poem) is always historical and addresses a historical community. Mexico and the poem thus become, for Paz, two articulations of being in the world: what the two texts explore is how that relation is expressed and to be read. In other words, how the literary reads community and community reads the poem.

ON EXEMPLARITY: *EL LABERINTO DE LA SOLEDAD*

In *El laberinto de la soledad* Paz puts the contiguity between nation and being in question. Even as he declares that "nadie puede explicar satisfactoriamente en qué consisten las diferencias 'nacionales' entre argentinos y uruguayos, peruanos y ecuatorianos, guatelmatecos y mexicanos" [no one can satisfactorily explain the "national" differences between Argentineans and Uruguayans, Peruvians and Ecuadorians, Guatemalans and Mexicans] (123), (the frontiers between these nations being the product of the political expediency of post-independence partitioning), Paz will seek to describe what he calls the singularity of the Mexican (man or woman). *El laberinto de la soledad* thus seems to continue the tradition of the "ensayo del ser nacional" which, as we saw with Martínez Estrada, seeks to delineate the particularity of national belonging. Paz himself makes the continuity of this tradition explicit when, at the beginning of the essay, he states: "Basta, por ejemplo, con que cualquiera cruce la frontera para que, obscuramente, se haga las mismas preguntas que se hizo Samuel Ramos en *El perfil del hombre y la cultura en México*" (LS 49) [It is enough, for example, simply to cross the border: almost at once we begin to ask ourselves, at least vaguely, the same questions that Samuel Ramos asked in his *Profile of Man and Culture in Mexico* (12)].

The inclusion of Ramos's text is strategic for Paz. Although written abroad, *El laberinto de la soledad* is a response to a topic that dominated the Mexican cultural context at the time: the so-called "filosofía de lo mexicano" [philosophy of Mexican-ness]. Following the lead of Ramos's book of 1934 as well as the teachings of the Spanish philosopher José Gaos, these writers sought to define the Mexican essence.[4] In *Posdata* (1970), first presented as the Hackett Memorial Lecture at the University of Texas, Austin, Paz explains that the intent of *El laberinto de la soledad* "fue un ejercicio de la imaginación crítica: una visión y, simultáneamente, una revisión. Algo muy distinto a un ensayo sobre la filosofía de lo mexicano o a una búsqueda de nuestro pretendido ser. El mexicano no es una esencia sino una historia . . . En aquella época no me interesaba la definición de lo mexicano sino, como ahora, la crítica: esa actividad que consiste, tanto o más que en conocernos, en liberarnos"[5] [was an exercise of the critical imagination: a vision and, simultaneously, a revision—something very different from an essay on Mexican-ness or a search for our supposed being. The Mexican is not an essence but a history . . . In those days I was not interested in a definition of Mexican-ness but rather, as now, in criticism: that activity which consists not only in knowing ourselves but, just as much or more, in freeing ourselves (215–16)].

Paz's critique of nationalist interpretations of Mexican history also responds to the post-war view on the decline of the concept of the Nation-State and the pernicious effects of the nationalism of Nazi Germany. Working as a correspondent for the Mexican magazine *Mañana* in 1945, Paz writes: "Ahora empieza una nueva era;

el Estado nacional depende cada vez más de los otros Estados y ya
no es posible hablar de una política nacionalista sin demagogia"
[Now a new era begins; the Nation-State depends more and more
on other States and it is no longer possible to speak of a nationalist
politics without demagoguery] and "El nacionalismo agresivo de
hace 20 años ha desaparecido. Los pueblos no sólo demandan una
mejor distribución de las riquezas; quieren fundamentalmente una
mejor organización internacional"[6] [The aggressive nationalism of
20 years ago has disappeared. The People not only demand a better
distribution of wealth; they fundamentally want a better international organization]. For Paz, Mexican history in the post-war period can be approached only through a critique of nationalist
definitions of Mexican-ness and by proposing the universalizing
thrust of Mexican singularity. It is for this reason that *El laberinto
de la soledad* begins with a discussion of a type of interpretation of
the nation that in post-war Mexico is no longer valid.

Indeed, if Samuel Ramos and his disciples sought to define and
thus delimit the meaning of being Mexican, that is, if in "la filosofía de lo mexicano" there was a substantive positing of Mexican
identity, in his essay Paz will attempt to problematize what is at
stake in the need to define the "national character": "A pesar de la
naturaleza casi siempre ilusoria de los ensayos de psicología nacional, me parece reveladora la insistencia con que en ciertos períodos
los pueblos se vuelven sobre sí mismos y se interrogan" (LS 47)
[Despite the often illusory nature of essays on the psychology of a
nation, it seems to me there is something revealing in the insistence
with which a people will question itself (9–10)]. However, in lieu
of defining the national "being," in lieu of fixing its place, Paz will
opt to develop a form of writing which attempts to interrupt the presuppositions of the quest of identity. In the very exposition of *El
laberinto de la soledad*, as well as in the discussion of poetry in *El
arco y la lira*, Paz's intent is to avoid the politics of identity thinking which are intrinsic to the "filosofía de lo mexicano."

Part of the strategy of *El laberinto de la soledad* is rhetorical and
lies in eschewing the notion of defining in favor of providing examples.[7] As we will see, these examples will preclude any notion of
closure, a strategy that will, on the one hand, threaten the initial
purpose of the essay—to describe *the* Mexican particularity (what
makes a Mexican a Mexican)—but will also, on the other hand,
present the aporias of any search of identity and, therefore, of its
political implications.

Although conventionally conceived as conduits or mediums for the exposition of a truth or Truth, the examples will show not only their own limits but also those they are supposed to be examples *of.* The example thus complicates the rhetorical level of the text, as well as the conceptual framework that serves as the basis of that rhetoric. Since Plato and Aristotle, the example (from the Latin *exemplar*) has been associated with two vectors of meaning. The example can be a particular case of a universal form or model, the standard, the law itself; the example thus points to the problem of paradigm, source and origin, on the one hand, but also to that of parts, of practical and pragmatic functions, on the other.[8]

It is this sense of example that the Latin etymology *eximere* (a part taken out of some whole; in English, "exemption") emphasizes. How does the part stand for the whole and, similarly, how is the whole of which the example is a part constituted? What makes an example exemplify, represent, exhibit, stand for, not as a symbol or analogue but as illustration, an aid in understanding, visualizing? Does it draw its power from what it is a part of, or is there a power in the part itself, in the part as part?[9] Further, are examples always successful or can examples fail? That is, what happens when the nexus that is supposed to tie the general law, source, or model to the example comes apart? Would it be possible for them to switch places?

The example is always ambiguous then because it can function both as an undistinguished sample and as a teleological model, as a singular instance and as universal paragon. The aporetic nature of the example is present in the very first line of *El laberinto de la soledad*: "A todos, en algún momento, se nos ha revelado nuestra existencia como algo particular, intransferible y precioso" (47) [All of us, at some moment, have had a vision of our existence as something unique, untransferable and very precious (9)]. One's singular existence is also everyone's singular existence in the sense that everyone ("todos") experiences life singularly. Does this characteristic shared by all human beings imply a "we"? Can it function as an example of the universal commonality of experience or, rather, are "we" all singular atoms, as *Webster's Dictionary* indicates ("we" is defined as "I" plus the rest of the group)? Further, does the "todos" of the first line of the essay necessarily point to all human beings or to the totality (however that may be defined) of the Mexican population?[10] Can the universal also be said to have limits?

The problem of the example points to the irreducible relation between the concepts of universalism and particularism. Indeed, a discussion of these concepts is a major component of *El laberinto de la soledad*, not only as they pertain to the problem of identity, but also to a discussion of the problem of modernity. Paz provides a frame for thinking these questions—the example given in the epigraph by Antonio Machado: "la incurable otredad que padece lo uno" [the incurable otherness which oneness must always suffer]. The goal of the essay then seems to be clear: the task for Paz is to distinguish the singularity of the Mexican as other, without making an essence of that singularity. That is, without making of Mexican identity an essential and essentializing foundation but, rather, some thing which is open to the movement of history.

Paz proposes to do this "by example," by showing that those elements that supposedly foreground a Mexican particularity (myths, customs, beliefs, traditions: what makes a Mexican Mexican) are always a mask of its being. Does this mean then that Paz already knows what being Mexican means and seeks only to enlighten his readers? How can an example of what cannot be properly represented (of what is masked) be given? Shouldn't examples be representations which aid in understanding, a pedagogical tool used in order to "visualize" what would otherwise be incomprehensible? Can a non-representable example be an example? If so, what would it be an example of?

Paz frames the writing of *El laberinto de la soledad* as a necessity.[11] Young nations, he states, will always be concerned about their identity: "¿qué somos y cómo realizaremos eso que somos?" (47) [What are we, and how can we fulfill our obligations to ourselves as we are (9)]. Even though a "we" is implied in the questions he poses, the concern with national identity will yield a partial or incomplete study, Paz informs his readers: "No toda la población que habita nuestro país es objeto de mis reflexiones, sino un grupo concreto, constituido por esos que, por razones diversas, tiene conciencia de su ser en tanto que mexicanos. Contra lo que se cree, este grupo es bastante reducido" (48) [My thoughts are not concerned with the total population of our country, but rather with a specific group made up of those who are conscious of themselves, for one reason or another, as Mexicans (11)]. Paradoxically, Paz's essay seeks to delineate Mexican particularity (and thus respond to the question "¿qué somos?" [what are we?], but simultaneously posits that the essay will concern itself with those for whom that particularity is already a conscious reality. What is the relation then between the universal "todos" of the first line who feel the singularity of their being and the particular "no toda" of the Mexican population? If "everyone" at some time feels the singularity of his/her being, why can't this also be true of the "everyone" implied in the Mexican population and not only a small group?

Positing the problems that the essay will tackle in this manner allows Paz to maintain the notions of universality, as well as of particularity, open and incomplete. The universal is not given a particular body, a substantive identification, and the particular is in turn not made into a universal. The tension inhabiting the notion of example is unresolved, necessarily incomplete. This incompleteness will allow both concepts to be put in relation as a future goal and promise: "Todos pueden llegar a sentirse mexicanos" (49) [Everyone can one day feel Mexican].

This last affirmation seems to answer the question posed by Paz of how the community can be thought once the notion of totality has been put in question. That is, when confronted with "una oscura conciencia de que hemos sido arrancados del Todo y una ardiente búsqueda: una fuga y un regreso, tentativa por restablecer los lazos que nos unían a la creación" (LS 49) [an obscure awareness that we have been torn from the All, and an ardent search: a flight and a return, an effort to re-establish the bonds that united us with creation (20)]. Unable to anchor his discourse in the centrality of a transcendental certainty (God, the Subject, the universal embodied in the European ideal), Paz is aware that the notion of ground has been disrupted, as well as those concepts which presupposed the stability of that ground. Yet he insists on revisiting notions concerned with authenticity, origins, even as he is aware that a thinking of identity which is self-grounded is "superflua y peligrosa" (LS 47) [pointless and even dangerous (10)]. Paz will therefore call for thinking the other of identity, not as a property or a new subject, but as what is permanently destabilizing and unrepresentable.

Paz faces a difficult task in *El laberinto de la soledad*: he must posit a "being Mexican" which is open to the universal while not making of that universal another identity (hasn't this been the objective of totalitarian or imperialist projects?). The movement of the "todos" in the first chapter of *El laberinto de la soledad* complicates the notion of a binary relation between national particularity and human universality. The "todos" of the first line can now be seen to have been transmuted into a universality in the Mexican and one could say that this is precisely the goal of the essay: to be able to inscribe the universal in a so-called national particularity and vise versa.[12]

If Paz's essay constantly waivers between the law (the model, the universal) and the example (the particular, the unique), it is because, as we have seen, examples are always double: they can answer to the law (however that law may be defined) and to an other law (or to the law of the other), to what cannot be generalized or even represented. In other words, examples can function to institute the law (they are thus examples *of* the law) and to displace it.[13] A constitutive undecidability seems to be at the heart of *El laberinto de la soledad* and, as we will see, this undecidability is crucial for Paz's rethinking of the notion of identity.

The aporetic nature of examples becomes evident in Paz's description of young Mexican Americans living in Los Angeles, the *pachucos*, which makes up the first chapter of the essay. Even though Paz states that his study will be concerned with that part of the population which already possesses national consciousness, his analysis begins with those for whom being Mexican is a problem, even a matter of life and death, those who "no reivindican su raza ni la nacionalidad de sus antepasados" (LS 50) [do not attempt to vindicate their race or the nationality of their forebears (14)].[14] Why begin the essay with the case of the *pachucos* who put the law of national belonging (of Mexican-ness) in question; that is, with those who are not exemplary? In order to interrogate the singularity of being Mexican, Paz will begin his analysis with an exception to the rule: the example as a part cut from the whole. Although Paz never specifies what the whole is, the *pachuco*—for now—will be the part.

The situation of the *pachuco* in Paz's schema is that of the adolescent who, like Narcissus, begins to develop self-consciousness. Analogously, it is also that of young countries in "trance de crecimiento" [critical moment of development]. The *pachuco* then will be an example of both a singularity (of a consciousness, to use Paz's words) and of a nation. In the in-betweeness of the *pachuco* Paz reads the aporias of the problem of identity as well as that of being in the world: he is unable both to affirm a self-engendering identity as well as to make of the North American an absolute other, since in his hostile, aggressive stance toward the Unites States, the *pachuco* affirms the very identity he is trying to negate.

The *pachucos* are thus caught in an oppositional relation with respect to both Mexican and North American culture. In Paz's schema the *pachucos* answer to two laws and seem open to a certain plurality that has no ultimate particularity. Being extreme cases, hence the title of the first chapter:,"El *pachuco* y otros extremos" [The *Pachuco* and Other Extremes], they seem to defy the law of nationality. That is, the situation of the *pachucos* allows them the "liberty" of not having to be the particular case of a homogenous series. Yet precisely because of their non-exemplarity, the *pachucos* are also caught up in the same dialectical relation as "los otros" [the others], who in this case are the rest of the Mexicans, as well as the North Americans who, though differently, are also unable to express their true being. *Pachucos*, Mexicans, and North Americans thus share "nuestra común incapacidad para reconciliarnos con el fluir de la vida"[15] [our common incapacity to reconcile ourselves with the flux of life] (58).

The case of the *pachucos* points to a certain incompleteness in the example: it does and does not serve to exemplify a law; it is and is not properly unique; it does and does not answer to a model.[16] In this way, Paz is able to point to the aporias of identity thinking and avoid making of the "descriptions" of the "Mexican" that he provides in the essay a stable or static entity, an essence. If there are Mexican particularities, then they will be an always-receding horizon. The incompleteness of the example or what one could call its failure (its inability to successfully illustrate or demonstrate what it is an example *of*) points to a notion of "demonstration" not tied to a concept of ultimate Truth. That is, if examples can be said to be at the heart of the logic of modernity (so many examples toward an ultimate progression in the attainment of Truth), then Paz's examples question this logic by complicating and thus undermining the teleological presuppositions of exemplarity.[17]

It is important to note, however, that Paz himself cannot avoid making of the *pachuco* an exemplary case and thus answerable to some law, given that in his very commonality with Mexicans and North Americans, he necessarily becomes one more example (now in a series) of the solitude of man. Like everyone ("todos"), he is also alone. The *pachuco* allows Paz to begin to develop the dialectic solitude-communion ("soledad-comunión"), a dialectic which, despite the eschatological implications of the notion of communion, retains the negativity of dialectical movement while dispensing with the sublation into Absolute Knowledge which is central to the Hegelian version.[18]

MYTH AND COMMUNITY

In the first section of *El laberinto de la soledad* Paz contends that any singularity (however it may be named) is always open to the outside and, therefore, always incomplete, unable to close in on itself and become a self-engendering identity. Given this situation, the following three chapters of the essay appear problematic since here Paz points to a notion of Mexican-ness that the first chapter on the *pachucos* seemed to question. Time and time again, Paz calls attention to a particular Mexican way of confronting death, the body, ritual (or celebrations), the use of language, etc. Is Paz contradicting himself? Is there, after all, a Mexican particularity that could also be termed its essence or foundation?

In his 1970 interview with Claude Fell, Paz notes: "[yo] creo que *El laberinto* fue una tentativa por describir y comprender ciertos mitos"[19] [I think that *The Labyrinth of Solitude* was an attempt to describe and understand certain myths (334)]. Although not the focus of the entire essay, in the chapters titled "Máscaras mexicanas," [Mexican Masks] "Todos Santos, Día de Muertos" [The Day of the Dead] and "Los hijos de la Malinche," [The Sons of La Malinche] Paz does describe and analyze certain myths and by so doing again presents a paradoxical situation. Myth is traditionally defined as deriving "of and from the origin, it relates back to a mythic foundation and through this relation it founds itself (a consciousness, a people, a narrative)."[20] One of the principal preoccupations of the essay is with origins: "la historia de Mexico es la del hombre que busca su filiación, su origen, . . . restablecer los lazos" [the history of Mexico is that of a man who seeks his parentage, his origin . . . to re-establish ties] (54). Yet the myths which supposedly "explain" Mexican particularity (the myth of Cuauhtémoc, la Malinche, etc.) and should serve as the very foundation of the Mexican community, are shown to no longer perform their mythic function in the essay. They are thus reduced, in Paz's formulation, to symptoms, to manifestations (celebrations of certain holidays, the use of language, such as the verb "chingar," violent outbursts, etc): degraded and fragmentary forms of what "previously" held the community together or through which communion was achieved.[21]

The manifestations of myth in *El laberinto* are able to enact the dialectic solitude-communion, although myth itself would not be thought dialectically. In their manifestations of myth, the "Mexican" approaches but is unable to "saltar el muro de la soledad" [cross the wall of solitude] and "no trasciende su soledad" [does not transcend his solitude] (74, 88). If myth is always the myth of a communion, of the "unique voice of the many," then Paz finds in the Mexican experience no such possibility of transcendence, only "efímeras representaciones" [ephemeral representations] (75) which occur during certain celebrations or "efímera trascendencia" [ephemeral transcendence] (83), as when committing a crime. At these times, Mexicans are able to open themselves up to the outside ("abrirse") and thus allow for the experience of otherness.

Even though Paz subscribes to the notion of revealing vestiges of mythic life as a way to break with the dialectic solitude-communion, he must also necessarily interrupt that mythic residue and appeal to a notion of otherness ["otredad"] that seems to put in question the very survival of myth. If myth is founded and founds community by appealing to substantive positings of completed identity (all in one) and identification—and for this reason myth is important for nationalisms which are founded on organic ideologies of blood and soil—then any appeal to otherness, to what disturbs the self-generation and self-identification of the community, also disturbs the very function of myth.

One could say that this double movement in the essay (the recuperation as well as the impossibility of fully realizing mythic function) is typical of any modern formulation of community, given that modernity (its legitimization, as well as its critique) also depends on a notion of myth.[22] It is important to note, however, that just as in his analysis of the *pachucos*, Paz's double movement in the chapters on the manifestation of myths allows the notions of both singularity and totality (or particularity and universality) to remain open and incomplete, in tension; something that the totalizing notion of myth cannot do. Mythic discourse or speech ignores the question of singular existence and, as we saw in the section on the *pachucos*, singularity is a central category in Paz's formulations.

As in the first chapter on the *pachucos*, then, the chapters on myth in *El laberinto de la soledad* both inscribe and interrupt the notion of exemplarity. If myth signals what is properly unique to a community and makes of that uniqueness a universal law that holds the community together, then the manifestations of myth among Mexicans are both particular and improper. They provide a myth of origins, but are unable to hold the community together as one.

The inscriptions and interruptions of myths in Paz's essay seek to produce a writing on Mexico and Mexicans that differs from the tradition of "la filosofía de lo mexicano" [the philosophy Mexican-ness] and its essentializing notion of national identity. More recently critics have returned to the problems of particularity and universality in order to problematize the concept of identity, and because the terms of the debate are similar to those employed by Paz in *El laberinto de la soledad,* it is worthwhile to note the implications that these critics draw from a discussion of these concepts in order to understand the continued import of Paz's essay of 1959.[23]

Ernesto Laclau notes that the so-called "death of the Subject" generated an interest in subjectivities and how identities are constituted. While Laclau sees this as a fortuitous situation (allowing for the amplification of the political field necessary for a radical democracy), he is also attentive to the dangers of a proliferation of differential identities. For this reason Laclau shows how the notion of identity (or particularity) cannot be thought apart from a thinking of universality. If it is not to become totalizing and repressive, the concept of identity must remain incomplete and be inhabited by what Laclau calls, following psychoanalytic theory, a constitutive lack.[24] This lack opens itself up to the universal by not allowing an identity to become complete, thus exposing it to an endless series of identifications.[25] A radical democratic politics must leave the paradoxical relation between the universal and particular intact, according to Laclau:

> The universal . . . does not have a concrete content of its own (which would close it on itself), but is an always receding horizon resulting from the expansion of an indefinite chain of equivalent demands. The conclusion seems to be that universality is incommensurable with any particularity but cannot, however, exist apart from the particular . . . The solution of the paradox would imply that a particular body had been found, which would be the true body of the universal.[26]

In Laclau's formulation both the universal and the particular are exposed to an otherness that does not allow either of them to become full (to close in on themselves) nor be subsumed one by the other. The tension between the two concepts is thus never resolved.[27]

Paz's question in *El laberinto de la soledad*: "¿cómo crear una sociedad, una cultura, que no niegue nuestra humanidad pero tampoco la convierta en una vana abstracción? [how should a society and a culture that do not negate our humanity or covert it into a vain abstraction be created?] (176) speaks to the irreducible relation between the universal and the particular that Laclau formulates in his text.[28] Re-stated in the terms we have been using throughout this chapter, one could say that a particular case or example cannot stand apart from the universal or general law, but neither can it be reduced to it. The example would thus be what both allows and disavows exemplarity, not because the exemplary ceases to exist, but rather because it can no longer exist as an essence or a foundation. Such a formulation allows us to think the notions of singularity and plurality as not bound to the presuppositions of an absolute individuality, nor of an essential commonality.[29] One can now see the import of Paz's formulation of Mexican identity which he states in the first chapter of *El laberinto de la soledad*: "Todos pueden llegar a sentirse mexicanos" [Everyone can one day feel Mexican]. Stated as a promise and as a feeling (not as an axiom or theory), the community appears as that which is exposed in the act of coming together, but not as an already completed totality, nor as an origin or a foundation.

THE (IM) POSSIBILITY OF POETRY: *EL ARCO Y LA LIRA*

La poesía no dice: yo soy tú; dice: mi yo eres tú. La imagen poética es la otredad.

[Poetry does not say: I am you; it says: My I is you. The poetic image is otherness.
                              —O. Paz, "Los signos en rotación" ["Signs in Rotation"]

Does poetry function as the unique example of community in Paz's texts, the exemplary site for the collective? In his writings of the 1930s and 1940s Paz had already signaled poetry's ability to reveal "lo mexicano"[30] and at one level *El arco y la lira* seems to follow the Heidegger of "Hölderlin and the Essence of Poetry" in declaring the anteriority of poetic language to ordinary, everyday speech and its originary foundational role for the historical community:[31]

El poema se nutre del lenguaje vivo de una comunidad, de sus mitos, sus sueños y sus pasiones, esto es, de sus tendencias más secretas y poderosas. El poema funda al pueblo porque el poeta remonta la corriente del lenguaje y bebe en la fuente original. En el poema la sociedad se enfrenta con los fundamentos de su ser, con su palabra primera. (AL 67).[32]

[The poem feeds on the living language of a community, on its myths, its dreams and its passions, that is, its strongest and most secret tendencies. The poem founds the people because the poet retraces the course of language and drinks from the original source. In the poem society is face to face with the foundations of its existence, with its initial word (30).]

The poem thus becomes the voice of the community: the repository of the People's original word and, most importantly, a source and site of communion. The language of the poem and of the People are one. Paz's assertion here seems to indicate that the poem overcomes the dialectical relation that the essayist posited in *El laberinto de la soledad* between solitude and communion. Following Heidegger's view on poetic essence, the poem would seem to resolve that agonistic relation:[33]

Dos fuerzas antagónicas habitan el poema: una de elevación o desarraigo, arranca a la palabra del lenguaje; otra de gravedad, que la hace volver. El poema es creación original y única, pero también es lectura y recitación: participación. El poeta lo crea; el pueblo, al recitarlo, lo recrea . . . Las dos operaciones—separación y regreso—exigen que el poema se sustente en un lenguaje común . . . en la lengua de una comunidad: ciudad, nación, clase, grupo o secta. (AL 65)

[Two opposing forces inhabit the poem: one of elevation or uprooting, which pulls the word from the language; the other of gravity, which makes it return. The poem is an original and unique creation, but it is also reading and recitation: participation. The poet creates it; the people, by recitation, re-create it . . . The two operations—separation and return—require that the poem be sustained by a common language . . . by the language of a community: city, nation, class, group or sect (28).]

Yet even though the passage posits the sharing of a common language between poet and reader (or public), the tension between alienation and reconciliation, the agonistic relation in the poem itself, is not resolved ("Dos fuerzas antagónicas *habitan* el poema" [Two opposing forces *inhabit* the poem], my emphasis); the tension between the two forces remains a constitutive element of the poem.

The apparent contradiction in the above two quotes expresses, according to Enrico M. Santí, a certain vacilation in *El arco y la lira* between a humanist conception of the subject (and therefore, of creation, consciousness, reason, of the voice as presence, etc.) and the disseminating movement of writing.[34] Throughout the essay one can indeed find examples to support both theoretical stands. However, I would sustain that far from being a theoretical slippage on the part of Paz (an indecision regarding the presuppositions of a surrealist existentialism and those of structuralism, both of which inform the theoretical framework of the essay), the undecidability in the essay points to that tension which poetry embodies for Paz and for which no resolution can be found.[35] The undecidability that Santí registers in Paz would thus come to confirm the limits, the impossibilities, as well as the possibilities of what Paz calls the poetic image.

The differences that for Paz distinguish poetry from the poet are one way to approach the issue of undecidability. In *El arco y la lira* the poet is associated, at times, with creation, with voice, with presence; at others, he is in a perpetual exile. Although the poet must share the language of the community, the place of the poet is uncertain. The poet for Paz is a "desterrado," one who is (literally) without ground. This situation cannot be otherwise: "si el poeta abandona su destierro . . . abandona también la poesía y la posibilidad de que ese exilio se transforme en comunión" (67)[36] [If the poet abandons his exile . . . he also abandons poetry and the possibility that this exile will be transformed into communion (31)]. For Paz the poet can only be so called if he is permanently dis-located; communal fusion would signal the death toll of the poet and poetry.

In light of the poet's exile, the notion of poetic language is also complicated because the language that the poet utilizes to write his poem is never truly his (he is not the language's creator). The poet is rather a "servidor del lenguaje" [servant of language] given that "el artista no se sirve de sus instrumentos—piedras, sonido, color or palabra—como el artesano, sino que los sirve para que recobren su naturaleza original" (AL 49) [the artist is not served by his tools—stone, sound, color or word—like the artisan, but serves them to recover their original nature (13)]. Paradoxically, the poet becomes the product of the poetic work, not its creator, thereby complicating notions of origins, of hierarchy, and of presence over absence. But perhaps more importantly, for Paz the poet must circumvent the law of exchange and, therefore, the instrumental use of language as a medium of power and control.

The essay's exposition of what Paz calls the poet's active passivity ("pasividad activa") also serves to problematize the notion of the Subject as substratum, as the voice of the community.[37] Paz does not do away with the concept of man (this would be a banality), but in *El arco y la lira* he does put in question the will to power and presence as the ultimate goal of man:

> El hombre pone en marcha el lenguaje. La noción de un creador, necesario antecedente del poema parece oponerse a la creencia en la poesía como algo que escapa al control de la voluntad. Todo depende de lo que se entienda por voluntad . . . Si no es posible trazar las fronteras entre el cuerpo y el espíritu, tampoco lo es discernir dónde termina la voluntad y empieza la pura pasividad . . . La abolición en estados de absoluta receptividad no implica la abolición del querer . . . El Nirvana ofrece la misma combinación de pasividad activa, de movimiento que es reposo. *Los estados de pasividad—desde la experiencia del vacío interior hasta la opuesta de congestión del ser—exigen el ejercicio de una voluntad dedicada a romper la dualidad entre objeto y sujeto . . . Todos sabemos hasta qué punto es difícil rozar las orillas de la distracción. Esta experiencia se enfrenta a las tendencias predominantes de nuestra civilización, que propone como arquetipos humanos al abstraído, al retraído y hasta al contraído. Un hombre que se distrae niega al mundo moderno. Al hacerlo, se juega el todo por el todo.* (AL 64), my emphasis.

> [Man sets language in motion. The notion of a creator, a necessary antecedent of the poem, seems to be opposed to the belief in poetry as something that escapes the control of the will. Everything depends on what is understood by will . . . If it is not possible to trace the limits between body and spirit, neither is it possible to discern where the will ends and pure passivity begins . . . Immersion in states of absolute receptivity does not imply the abolition of the will . . . Nirvana offers the same combination of active passivity, of movement that is repose. *States of passivity—from the experience of inner emptiness to the opposite one of congestion of being—require the exercise of a will determined to destroy the duality between object and subject . . . We all know how difficult it is to reach the shores of distraction. This experience runs counter to the prevailing tendencies of our civilization, which proposes abstraction, retraction, and even contraction as archetypes of human behavior. A man who is distracted denies the modern world. In doing this, he gambles everything.* (27), my emphasis]

The notion of "active passivity" is developed in Heidegger's "Hölderlin and the Essence of Poetry," where the German philosopher shows that the critic or commentator cannot interpret Being as it is transmitted in the poem; he must simply listen to it, "receive and preserve it." Paz will transcribe this notion in the following manner: "El poeta escucha. En el pasado fue el hombre de la visión. Hoy aguza el oído y percibe que el silencio mismo es voz, murmullo que busca la palabra de su encarnación. El poeta escucha lo que dice el tiempo, aun si dice: nada" [The poet listens. In the past he was the man of vision. Today he pricks up his ear and perceives that silence itself is voice, a murmur that seeks the word of its incarnation. The poet listens to what the time says, even if it says: nothing] (AL 272).[38] The poem does not communicate a message or information; the truth of its meanings is not to be deciphered as a representation and, therefore, the notion of interpretation, as well as of agency (of determining the bearer of the message) is also put in question.

Ultimately, though, it is the question of poetry and not of the poet which is at stake for Paz *in El arco y la lira*: "El poeta ya tiene un 'lugar' en la sociedad. ¿Lo tiene la poesía?" [The poet already has a "place" in society. Does poetry?](AL 67). The poet occupies a "place" for Paz if he becomes part of official culture, but it is poetry's ability or inability to escape the force of instrumental reason and thus "reveal" the being of the community that is the point in question here. In this sense, poetry does not have a place, for Paz; poetry cannot have a place in modern society, if by place we understand that which would be the object of a representation.

Paz's notion of the poetic image thus complicates the concept of place as modernity has defined it. According to Samuel Weber,

> What characterizes modernity since the Renaissance . . .—is not the fact that it substitutes one world-view for another but . . . that it defines itself through the attempt to conquer the world as image. . . . To determine the world as having the structure of a picture or image is thus to embark upon a project of conquest in which the heterogeneity of beings is accepted only insofar as it can be objectified and represented . . . [it is the] overriding aim of putting things in their place. . . . fixing things in place thereby confirms the place of the subject that, through the power to represent, becomes the "reference point of beings as such". When such a movement is understood as encompassing the totality of beings as such, the "world" itself has become a "picture" whose ultimate function is to establish and confirm the centrality of man as the being capable of depiction.[39]

Weber here summarizes the main thesis of Heidegger's "The Age of the World Picture,"[40] which shows how the modern proliferation of technology has resulted in the objectification of the world as representation (image or picture) and the establishment of man as Subject. The "conquest of the world as picture" indicates one of the last strongholds of metaphysics and of the calculable mastery of man over all that is. At the end of the essay, however, Heidegger shows how Hölderlin's poetry dislocates the subject-object duality and creates a "space withdrawn from representation."[41] Poetry becomes the only conduit toward the dis-placement of the heterogeneity of things called world and therefore an access to truth.

Paz appears to agree with Heidegger's insights but disputes the terms of the discussion. In "Los signos en rotación" [Signs in Rotation] the following observation is repeated in different forms throughout the short essay: "La técnica no es una imagen ni una visión del mundo: no es una imagen porque no tiene por objeto representar o producir la realidad; no es una visión porque no concibe al mundo como figura sino como algo más o menos maleable para la voluntad humana" and "La técnica es una realidad tan poderosamente real—visible, palpable, audible, ubicua—que la verdadera realidad ha dejado de ser natural o sobrenatural: la industria es nuestro paisaje, nuestro cielo y nuestro infierno" (AL 254) [Technology is neither an image nor a vision of the world: it is not an image because its aim is not to represent or reproduce reality; it is not a vision because it does not conceive the world as a figure but as a something more or less malleable to the human will] and [Technology is a reality so powerfully real—visible, palpable, audible, ubiquitous—that the real reality has ceased to be natural or supernatural: industry is our landscape, our heaven and our hell (241)].

Central to Paz's disagreement with Heidegger is that for the former technology does not present a totalizing structure in which meanings are generated—technology cannot provide a vision of the world—but is, rather, a series of functions, tools, and acts devoid of significance outside of their immediate use. In fact, for Paz, technology does not allow for a conception of "world" at all ("Ahora el espacio se expande y disgrega; el tiempo se vuelve discontinuo; y el mundo, el todo, estalla en añicos" AL 253) [Now space expands and breaks apart; time becomes discontinuous; and the world, the whole, explodes into splinters (240)], given technology's inability to produce images. The status of the image is therefore central to Paz's distance from Heidegger. As we will see, Paz associates the image only with poetry. Because it is the only way to break with the logic of representation, the subject-object duality imposed by modernity, the image allows for a thinking of alterity.

THE POETIC IMAGE

An elaboration of the notion of poetic image marks Paz's approach to the relation between poetry and communion. The image is the central problem of poetic (literary) language and lies at the heart of the question of modernity. In fact, it could be said that the nature of the image concerns the ways in which we apprehend the real, given that, since antiquity, its status and function mark the very relation between reality and imagination, the optical and the physical, the sensible and the aesthetic.[42]

As manuals and dictionaries attest, the image is difficult to define because of its ambiguous and oscillating position. The image can be both a direct substitution (as in a photographic image) and a mediated figuration (as in an analogical representation). This ambiguity led Maurice Blanchot to the following observation: "The image is an image in its duplicity, not the double of the object, but the initial unfolding [*dédoublement*] that henceforth permits the thing to be figured."[43] The image does not allow for the identity between subject and object; it puts this relation in question because the object cannot be traced back to an origin (as in the Romantic image), but rather to what is already doubled itself. For this reason, the image also complicates the notion of subject, given that specularity is not associated with the image. The classic example is that of Narcissus who sees himself in the reflection of the water, but does not recognize (identify) himself; Narcissus's image is altered beyond recognition.[44]

In *El arco y la lira*, the poetic image achieves "unity," "reconciliation," or "wholeness" at furtive and always disappearing moments. As in the analysis of the manifestations of myths in *El laberinto de la soledad* in which Paz shows how or when Mexicans are able to "transcend" their solitude, the "moment" of communion in poetry can only be an "instante relampagueante" [a flashing instant], an "instante de incandescencia" [an incandescent instant] or a "momentánea reconciliación" [a momentary reconciliation]; that is, an event which marks a presence but as a constantly disappearing present.

Similar to Benjamin's notion of *jetzseit* which makes the present emerge but "itself" remains unrepresentable,[45] Paz's poetic image "desafía el principio de contradicción" (AL 115) [challenges the principle of contradiction] and "abraza los contrarios" (AL 157) [welcomes contradictions]; the poetic image defies representation and thus the notion of identity: "El lenguaje traspasa el círculo de los significados relativos, el esto y el aquello, y dice lo indecible: las piedras son plumas, esto es aquello. El lenguaje indica, representa; el poema no explica ni representa, presenta" (AL 126) [Language goes beyond the circle of relative meanings, the this and the that, and it says the unsayable; stones are feathers, this is that. Language indicates, represents; the poem does not explain or represent: it presents (97)].

Paz's notion of "otredad" [alterity] is key for his problematization of the concept of representation. In Paz's poetic image "otredad" is the present's difference from itself, neither the homogenous repetition of historicist narratives nor modernity's faith in a never-ending future. For this reason the poetic image is what cannot be incorporated into an economy of signification and is thus associated in *El arco y la lira* with the sacred, with the other of reason, with dreams and the imagination, those elements which modernity's privileging of reason dismisses from its economy. That is why Paz asserts that poetry is neither judgment nor interpretation ("no puede aspirar a la verdad," "la imagen no explica" AL 115, 126) [it cannot aspire to truth, the image does not explain]. Poetry is not to be adjusted to a law, to beliefs: it is related to the order of the sacred, but not to that of religion. And because for Paz the poetic image defies institutional boundaries, it is excessive and thus a moment of liberation.[46]

To return to the question with which this chapter opened: is poetry the exemplary site of the collective, the "site" for community to be presented? One could say that, for Paz, poetry is the promise of community and because it "follows" the law of the other, it is also the non-exemplary example of a possibility:

La pregunta que se hace el poema—¿quién es el que dice esto que digo y a quién se lo dice?—abarca al poeta y al lector. La separación del poeta ha terminado: su palabra brota de una situación común a todos. No es la palabra de una comunidad sino de una dispersión; y no funda o establece nada, salvo su interrogación. Ayer, quizá, su misión fue "dar un sentido más puro a las palabras de la tribu"; hoy es una pregunta sobre ese sentido. Esa pregunta no es una duda sino una búsqueda. Y más es un acto de fe. No una forma sino unos signos que se proyectan en un espacio animado y que poseen múltiples significados posibles. El significado final de esos signos no lo conoce aún el poeta: está en el tiempo, el tiempo que entre todos hacemos y a que todos nos deshace. (AL 272)

[The question that the poem asks itself—who is he who says this that I say and to whom is it said?—embraces the poet and the reader. The poet's separation has ended: his word springs from a situation common to all. It is not the word of a community but of dispersion; and it does not found or establish anything, except its interrogation. Yesterday, perhaps, his mission was to give a purer sense to the words of the tribe; today it is a question about that sense. That question is not a doubt but a quest. And more: it is an act of faith. Not a form but some signs that are projected on an animated space and that possess multiple possible meanings. The poet does not yet know the final meaning of those signs: it is in time, the time we all make together and that unmakes us all. (262)]

Poetry for Paz cannot represent the truth of a community if by truth one understands the completed and total work of communion, but it can be a glimpse, an opening into the meanings of being in common. By foregrounding poetry's role in the dispute over sense, and not as that which assigns the final or proper sense of the community, Paz emphasizes poetry's essentially political role. Poetry's "sense" is fluid, multiple, and, above all, historical. Akin to Jacques Rancière's notion of disagreement where politics becomes possible in the poetic reconfiguration of terms in dispute, poetry in Paz thus becomes an "event" which interrupts the end/means rationality of official politics and allows for thinking the unthought or the previously unimaginable, for making and unmaking other forms of community.[47]

4

Borges: On Reading, Translation, and the Impossibility of Naming

Todo lenguaje es un alfabeto de símbolos cuyo ejercicio presupone un pasado que los interloctures *comparten.*

[Every language is an alphabet of symbols the employment of which assumes a past shared by its interlocutors.]
—J. L. Borges, "El aleph" ["The Aleph"]

IN REACTION TO THE VITRIOLIC ATTACKS ON THE INHUMAN AND FOR-eign nature of his writing, from the 1920s on Borges explores the question of a common language and its implications for the concept of literature.[1] Is there an authentic Argentinean language that would give rise to an equally authentic national literature? In "El idioma de los argentinos" (1927) [The Language of the Argentines] (1927), Borges responds to this question by referring to a double particularity: "Dos influencias antagónicas entre sí militan contra un habla argentina. Una es la de quienes imaginan que esa habla ya está prefigurada en el arrabalero de los sainetes; otra es la de los casticistas o españolados que creen en lo cabal del idioma y en la impiedad o inutilidad de su refacción"[2] [Two antagonistic influences battle against an Argentinean language. One is from those who imagine that the language is already prefigured in those who live in the margins of Buenos Aires and are represented in theater farces; the other is from the purists or pseudo-Spanish who believe in the accuracy of the language and in the impiety or uselessness of its modification]. Neither the localized slang of the Buenos Aires margins and its implied unity of place nor the linguistic cohesion of a dictionary Spanish that no one speaks succeeds in capturing the "voice" of the Spanish spoken in Argentina, crystallized as those two "languages" are by their proper and definite meaning.

If a certain cultural nationalism imposed the normalizing para-

95

meters that a pedagogical notion of an Argentinean essence embodied (the continuity with Hispanic tradition, the authenticity and
uniqueness that would mark the nation's autonomy), Borges finds
in the performative use of language a certain linguistic commonality: the "no escrito idioma argentino . . . *diciéndonos*" [the non-
written Argentinean language . . . speaking (to) us"] (IA 145),
where the intonation or inflection of certain words can be heard. In
"El aleph," and as the epigraph attests, he will refer to this commonality as sharing language.

Paradoxically what is common is not necessarily one's own as
indicated by the Spanish "share": "comparten" (from com-partir),
which points both to the commonality of experience and to the divi-
sion, splitting and distancing which that experience puts into play.
Sharing language thus destines the Argentinean writer to the task
of the translator, given that in the event that is writing, the voice,
the dialect (as Borges calls it) can never reach the unified stability
of a transparent national language.[3] The problem of translation that
sharing language demands and resists, the possibilities and impossibilities implied in transmitting, communicating or representing
sense, is Borges's approach to the question of a common language.

Does translation in Borges allow access to another space (or
realm), to another culture? Is anything transmitted in a Borgesean
translation? How should one think those moments in Borges's texts
when the translation is interrupted, where the transmission fails or,
as in "Emma Zunz," the characters speak two languages at the
same time: when there is no possibility of a translation taking
place? How should one think what escapes the translation process
and can only be thought as a non-localizable language? Writing
under the shadow of the two world wars, in "El aleph" and other
texts from the 1940s, Borges explores the relations between community and literature. Borges is especially concerned that the tenor
of that relation not subsume either of the two terms under peda-
gogic, normalizing and representational parameters, given that a
linguistic community can no longer assure the transmission of
sense. Borges's "shared" language thus proposes a writing that can
be considered Argentinean without having to be national.

Borges explicitly announces the impossibility of translation or
translation as an impossibility and writing of the limit in "Los traductores de las 1001 noches" ["The Translators of The Thousand
and One Nights"]: "Traducir el espíritu es una intención tan enorme y tan fantasmal que bien puede quedar como inofensiva; tra-

ducir la letra una precisión tan extravagante que no hay riesgo de
que la ensayen"[4] [To translate the spirit is so enormous and phan-
tasmal an intent that it may well be innocuous; to translate the letter, a requirement so extravagant that there is no risk of its ever
being attempted (95)]. The task of the translator is always a failure
for Borges. This does not mean that in Borges's texts there are no
translations or that he did not think them important, even invalu-
able. In fact, in various forms, translations or the task of translating
is a constant concern in his texts: "Ningún problema tan consustan-
cial con las letras y con su modesto misterio como el que propone
una traducción" [No problem is as consubstantial to literature and
its modest mystery as the one posed by translation] (69).[5] However,
despite its constant presence, translation in Borges's texts is not
simply considered an interlinguistic activity or, as some critics have
suggested, the strategy of an irreverent South American writer confronting Western culture.

Translation in Borges is considered a necessity for his writing,
for his task as a writer, while the materiality of his texts simultaneously announces and exposes its failure. As he states in "Las
versiones homéricas" ["The Homeric Versions"] (1932), it is impossible to know what belongs to the writer and what belongs to
language ("la dificultad categórica de saber lo que pertenece al
poeta y lo que pertenece al lenguage" [the categorical difficulty of
knowing what belongs to the poet and what belongs to language]
240). This impossibility resides in that between what language says
and the way it says it or, as Borges himself notes above, between
the intention and the precision, there is an abyss.[6] Translations expose this abyss, to which Borges's texts are also exposed.

A first approach to the problem of translation in Borges shows
that the notion of linguistic unity able to serve as the foundation for
a politics of the national community does not exist in his texts. This
lack of unity is contrasted to what, according to Borges, a certain
political discourse elected as the exemplary examples of cultural or
linguistic nationalism: the *Martín Fierro* (the so-called Argentinean
national poem) and the *Quixote* (the so-called monument to Hispa-
nism). In a lecture titled "El libro" ["The Book"] (1978) Borges
shows that in the selection of national poets, countries tend to exhibit a high level of arbitrariness. It is as if the national poet were
not exactly the one able to represent the characteristics of the nation's "spirit" but, rather, the one who emphasizes, denounces, and
declares, monstrously, the gap that exists between the imagination

and the so-called national community. Borges frames his commentary within the history of the concept of the book:

> Tenemos entonces un nuevo concepto, el de que cada país tiene que ser representado por un libro; en todo caso, por un autor que puede serlo de muchos libros. Es curioso—no creo que esto haya sido observado hasta ahora—que los países hayan elegido individuos que no se parecen demasiado a ellos. Uno piensa, por ejemplo, que Inglaterra hubiera elegido al doctor Johnson como representante; pero no, Inglaterra ha elegido a Shakespeare, y Shakespeare es—digámoslo así—el menos inglés de los escritores ingleses. Lo típico de Inglaterra es el understatement, es el decir un poco menos de las cosas. En cambio Shakespeare tendía a la hipérbole en la metáfora, y no nos sorprendería nada que Shakespeare hubiera sido italiano o judío, por ejemplo. Otro caso es el de Alemania; un país admirable, tan fácilmente fanático, elige precisamente a un hombre tolerante, que no es fanático y al que no le importa demasiado el concepto de patria; elige a Goethe . . . Otro caso más curioso es el de España. España está representada por Miguel de Cervantes. Cervantes es un hombre contemporáneo de la Inquisición, pero es tolerante, es un hombre que no tiene ni las virtudes ni los vicios españoles . . . Nosotros hubiéramos podido elegir el *Facundo* de Sarmiento . . . pero no, nosotros hemos elegido como libro la crónica de un desertor, hemos elegido el *Martín Fierro*, que si bien merece ser elegido como libro, ¿cómo pensar que nuestra historia está representada por un desertor de la conquista del desierto? . . . *Es como si cada país pensara que tiene que ser representado por alguien distinto, por alguien que pueda ser, una suerte de remedio, una suerte de triaca, una suerte de contraveneno de sus defectos.*[7] (my emphasis)

[We have a new concept according to which each country must be represented by a book or by an author of many books. It is curious—I do not think this has been noticed until now—that nations have chosen individuals who have little in common with them. One thinks, for example, that England would have chosen Doctor Johnson as it representative, but no, England has chosen Shakespeare, and Shakespeare is the least English of the English writers. The understatement is what is most typical of England—. But Shakespeare tended toward hyperbole in his metaphor, and it would not surprise us at all had Shakespeare been, for example, Italian or Jewish. Germany is another case, an admirable country, so easily fanatic yet it selects a tolerant man who is not a fanatic, and for whom the concept of nation is of little importance: Goethe. Another rather curious case is that of Spain. Spain is represented by Cervantes. Cervantes is a man contemporaneous to the Inquisition, but he is tolerant, he is a man who has neither the virtues nor the vices of Spain . . .

We could have chosen the *Facundo* by Sarmiento . . . but no, we chose as the book the chronicle of a deserter, we chose the *Martín Fierro*, which may well deserve being chosen as the book, but what should we make of the fact that our history is represented by a deserter of the conquest of the desert [i.e. the land of the indigenous people]? *It is as if each nation thought that it has to be represented by someone different, by someone who may be a kind of cure, a kind of antidote to its defects.* (my emphasis)]

Instead of facilitating the contiguity between language and community, for Borges the so-called national poem and book are symptoms of a problematic and imaginary relation. They seem to speak a foreign language, represent what the community does not want them to represent and do so in a style or a voice that is not properly that of the linguistic community. Indeed, the so-called national poet and book function within the logic of the *pharmakon*, which in Greek is defined not only as remedy (*triaca* and *contraveneno* are the words Borges utilizes) but is also defined as the poison itself.[8] If the national poet and book in Borges's text function as the imaginary remedy capable of curing the contradictions found within a supposed community's unity, they are also (literally) death itself ("la muerte") since they accentuate and exacerbate the gaps in that same national community and thus put in doubt the very unity they are supposed to represent.

The problem that Borges presents in "El libro" (that of a representation that in fact does not represent—or at least does not represent what it is supposed or intended to represent) is directly concerned with the problem of translation. And it is the term *pharmakon* itself that exposes this problem, given that if the Greek word can be translated as both remedy and poison it not only makes evident the problem of translating from one language to another but also that of translating within the language that one calls one's own. If within each linguistic system there are various languages, then one can no longer speak of a transparent non-contaminated language, one that is pure or intact. Neither can one any longer think that a translation consists in restituting in the translation what was first given in the original. That is, one can no longer think that the translation occupies a secondary or subaltern place in relation to the original—or that it even occupies a place.

We have learned from Walter Benjamin that translation cannot be thought within the genealogical line of heredity and similitude;

there are no family ties in translation, no natural relations. On the contrary, the translation and the so-called original are converted into the fragments of a "pure" language which is, at the same time, the impetus for translation (the dream of transparent communicability) and the greatest of impossibilities, since the multiplicity of languages does not permit the dream of transparency becoming a reality.[9]

The relation between translation and original for Benjamin, therefore, can only be an infinitely small point, a place which is in fact a non-place since it impedes unity or convergence and "exists" only in order to be abandoned. Translation in Benjamin, and also in Borges, is an orphaned translation. Because it rejects the place of the subaltern, it defies the law of the father, but also the law of the mother, of that motherland [madre patria] which could, if only for a moment, supply it with the reassuring site of an origin, with an identity.

"EL ALEPH": OF SPACES, PLACES, AND BEING IN COMMON

> Weak-minded people, beginning to think about the first letter of
> the alphabet, would rush into madness.
> —A. Rimbaud, "Letter to Paul Demeny, 15 May 1871,"*Works*

What does it mean to be an Argentinean writer? Variously defined as dependent on foreign (i.e. European) traditions (and thus cosmopolitan) or autonomous in relation to those traditions (and thus nationalist, although still negatively defined in relation to the "foreign"), the Argentinean writer either has too little or too much, is constantly in search of an identity to call his own or mourning the loss of one that was never properly his. This economy of gains and losses which has been the lot of most Latin American writers implies localizing the place that writer is supposed to occupy. Neither marginal, central nor "in-between," in "El aleph" (1941) Borges calls for a permanent dislocation of the writer and of writing.

In this story the mediocre poet Carlos Argentino Daneri reveals to Borges, the narrator, that he has found the Aleph (a point in space which contains all the other points). Daneri discovers the Aleph in the basement of his house on Garay Street and because of this discovery he is able to compose the epic poem later published as "Trozos argentinos" ["Argentine Fragments"] for which he is awarded the National Prize for Literature. If read only in reference to the intellectual politics of the time and to Borges's complicated relationship to Leopoldo Lugones, the story functions as a parody of Lugones's collection of poems, *Odas Seculares* [*Secular Odes*] (1910), which was written to commemorate the centenary of Argentina's Independence. Much like Daneri's poem, *Odas* pretends to give an encyclopedic account of the nation and therefore celebrates its plants, rivers, animals, and cities in an almost endless enumeration.[10] As in Daneri's *La Tierra* [*The Earth*], the poetic I in *Odas Seculares* also establishes a symbiotic and organic relation between nation and self, thus making the poet the natural representative and expression of the national community.[11]

It is well known that in 1941 Borges was not awarded the Municipal Prize for his entry "El jardín de senderos que se bifurcan" ["The Garden of Forking Paths"]. The jury considered Borges's work to be "extranjerizante," i.e. too imbued with foreign influences, a decision that the magazine *Nosotros* defended in 1942 with the following argument: "Si el jurado entendió que no podía ofrecer al pueblo argentino, en esta hora del mundo, con el galardón de la mayor recompensa nacional, una obra exótica y de decandencia . . . juzgamos que hizo bien" [If the jury understood that it could not offer the Argentinean people, at this point in time, the major national prize to an exotic and decadent work, . . . we judge that they did well].[12] There was a great deal of outrage among Borges's supporters—Borges was by then a well-known published writer—and "El aleph" can certainly be read in part as Borges's "revenge" on the members of the jury. No one would then have failed to recognize that the person whom Daneri chooses to write the prologue to his epic poem is none other than Alvaro Melián Lafinur. Having the same name as the character in the story, he was the only member of the jury to have voted in favor of Borges's story.

However, the central focus of "El aleph" is not only Borges's rejection of a certain type of nationalistic literature, but also the consequences of grounding literary production on the basis of a prior definition of national culture. More importantly, the story problematizes the possibilities and impossibilities for thinking the relation between literature and community, not as a theme or object of representation, but rather as what is enacted in the performative practice of writing. How should the "in common" be written, asks Borges, and with what language? Further, does the "in" in being in common presuppose a place, should it in order to enact the ethical and political dimensions of literature? If not, how can the problem of the meaning(s) of literature be thought?

"El aleph" has been read alongside Borges's essay "El escritor argentino y la tradición" ["The Argentinean Writer and Tradition"].[13] Accordingly, the story would confirm, in a fictionalized manner, the main thesis of the essay; namely, that even a subaltern Argentinean writer has access to the whole of Western tradition. In his comments on the essay, Ricardo Piglia frames Borges's thesis in the following manner: "¿Qué quiere decir la tradición argentina? Borges parte de esa pregunta y el ensayo es un manifiesto que acompaña la construcción ficcional de "El aleph", su relato sobre la escritura nacional. ¿Cómo llegar a ser universal en este suburbio del mundo?" [What does the Argentinean tradition mean? Borges begins with this question and the essay is a manifesto that accompanies its fictional version in "The Aleph," his story about national literature.] [14]

As a subaltern writer, Borges, according to Piglia, must necessarily define his position in relation to the central and hegemonic traditions that are both properly his (by virtue of his access through books) but of which he is dispossessed because of his marginal position in relation to those traditions (by virtue of being Argentinean):

La tesis central del ensayo de Borges es que las literaturas secundarias y marginales, desplazadas de las grandes corrientes europeas tienen la posibilidad de un manejo propio, "irreverente", de las grandes tradiciones . . . Pueblos de fronteras, que se manejan entre dos historias, en dos tiempos, y a menudo en dos lenguas. Una cultura nacional dispersa y fracturada, en tensión con una tradición dominante de alta cultura extranjera. Para Borges . . . este lugar incierto permite un uso específico de la herencia cultural.[15]

[The central thesis of Borges's essay is that, displaced from the great European trends, marginal and secondary literatures have the possibility of their own irreverent use of the great traditions . . . Countries on the border, that operate between two histories, two time frames and, frequently, between two languages. A national culture dispersed and fractured, in tension with the dominant tradition of a foreign high culture. For Borges . . . this uncertain place allows for a specific use of the cultural heritage.]

Although displaced (dispersed and fragmented) in relation to that center that for Piglia is represented by European culture, the secondary and marginal literatures are nevertheless able to produce specific uses of that central and centered tradition. Through what appears to be a strategy, a trick of the weak, the marginalized literatures in Piglia's schema thus assume a proper place (a place of their own) which is now the frontier.[16]

However, for this strategy to be possible, the categories Piglia employs depend on the prior unity of the differentiated spaces that are then placed in an oppositional relation: European/Argentinean, foreign/national, central/marginal, high culture/secondary, subaltern literature, although the first term in each of these relations appears to possess a fullness denied to the second.[17] The irreverence on the part of the subaltern writer depends on how he manages to bridge the gap or, better, to fill the void implied in these binary relations. He will be able to accomplish this goal, according to Piglia, by mixing, plagiarizing, or stealing from the hegemonic tradition those elements that are deemed useful or allow for an access or potentiality ("un llegar a ser") in his writing that would otherwise be impossible to achieve.

Borges's "El escritor argentino y la tradición" also depends on spatial metaphors for its exposition but, as we will see, these function differently than the theses that Piglia posits in his text. Everything in the essay intends to show the lack of unity and contiguity in what cultural nationalism defines as properly Argentinean and properly foreign. Regarding the supposed blood relations that certain critics claim to exist between Argentinean and Spanish literatures, that is, the linguistic unity which is supposed to be their common ground, Borges replies that Spanish literature is "hard to enjoy" (difícilmente gustable). To the claim that *Don Segundo Sombra* is the most essentially Argentinean of novels, Borges responds that it would not be so if the marks of the French literary tradition and Kipling's *Kim* were not inscribed in Güiraldes's writing.

As in his lecture "El libro", throughout "El escritor argentino y la tradición" Borges contends that in order to "communicate" the flavor of a certain country the text must be inscribed with a mark of difference, the text must be improper and this impropriety or difference must function at the level of the name:[18]

Durante muchos años, en libros ahora felizmente olvidados, traté de redactar el sabor, la esencia de los barrios extremos de Buenos Aires; naturalmente abundé en palabras locales, no prescindí de palabras como cuchilleros, milonga, tapia y otras . . . luego, hará un año, escribí una historia que se llama *La muerte y la brújula* que es una suerte de pesadilla, una pesadilla en que figuran elementos de Buenos Aires deformados por el horror de la pesadilla; pienso allí en el Paseo Colón y lo llamo Rue de Toulon; pienso en las quintas de Adrogué y las llamo Triste-le-Roy; publicada esa historia, mis amigos me dijeron que al fin habían encontrado en lo que yo escribía el sabor de las afueras de Buenos Aires. Precisamente porque no me había propuesto encontrar ese sabor, porque me había abandonado al sueño, pude lograr, al cabo de tantos años, lo que antes busqué en vano.[19]

[For many years, in books now happily forgotten, I tried to compose the flavor, the essence of the outskirts of Buenos Aires; naturally I abounded in local words such as *chuchilleros*, *milonga*, *tapia*, and others . . . then, about a year ago, I wrote a story called "Death and the Compass," which is a kind of nightmare, a nightmare in which elements of Buenos Aires appear, deformed by the horror of the nightmare; and in that story, when I think of the Paseo Colón, I call it Rue de Toulon; when I think of the *quintas* of Adrogué, I call them Triste-le-Roy; after the story was published, my friends told me that at last they had found the flavor of the outskirts of Buenos Aires in my writing. Precisely because I had not sought to find that flavor, because I had abandoned myself to the dream, I was able to achieve, after so many years, what I once sought in vain. (424, translation modified)]

Borges shows that there is no logical, direct or natural relation between imagination and nomination. No analogy of any sort can be established in the passage from Paseo Colón to Rue de Toulon; one is not the metaphor of the other. In fact between what is meant (Paseo Colón, Argentina) and the way that language means (Rue de Toulon) there is a non-relation that nevertheless succeeds in capturing the "flavor" (el sabor) of that order of signification.[20] In "La muerte y la brújula" writing works as something other to the translation process and yet retains, as Benjamin notes, an infinitely small yet unrepresentable point that is able to produce sense.

It is when the attempt to control language fails, when a literal, word by word translation is abandoned, that something of the original can be communicated. In other words, there is no way to make the intention and the name coincide. Indeed, the difference between imagination and nomination is transmitted as if in a dream, according to Borges, or, rather, a nightmare ("el horror de la pesadilla"), when the writer gives himself up with abandon and succumbs to the other of reason. This implies leaving something behind but also giving himself up to errancy: "porque me había abandonado al sueño, pude lograr . . . lo que antes busqué en vano" [because I had abandoned myself to the dream, I was able to achieve . . . what I once sought in vain] (EA 271). For Borges, then, the Argentinean writer can only be called by that name when he abandons himself, leaves himself behind, so to speak, or, if calling upon other senses of "abandonado" (linked to orphanhood and even bastardy) is someone outside the legality of the family structure. Writing thus implies giving up before the law, not in order to obey its letter (or to lay down another law), but rather to let the letter wander, never reaching its destination: a proper and definite meaning.[21]

The abandonment of the Argentinean writer results in his becoming permanently dis-appropriated, like the Jews or the Irish: "muchos de esos irlandeses ilustres (Shaw, Berkeley, Swift) fueron descendientes de ingleses, fueron personas que no tenían sangre celta: sin embargo, les bastó el hecho de sentirse irlandeses, distintos, para innovar en la cultura inglesa" [many of these illustrious Irishmen (Shaw, Berkeley, Swift) were the descendants of Englishmen, men with no Celtic blood; nevertheless, the fact of feeling themselves to be Irish, to be different, was enough to enable them to make innovations in English culture (426)] (EA 273). It is therefore *not* the right to the acquisition of the Western tradition by a marginal Argentinean writer that is at stake for Borges but, rather, the permanent destabilization of what is understood to be the property of the proper name (whether this name be Europe, Ireland, France, or Argentina): "no podemos concretarnos a lo argentino para ser argentinos" [we cannot confine ourselves to what is Argentine in order to be Argentine (427)] (EA 274). There is always something that exceeds nomination, which the name cannot contain and, to return to the passage I quoted earlier, it is for this reason that Paseo Colón can be translated into Rue de Toulon. Instead of designating the most concrete and unique of places, the translation of these "proper" names undoes the specificity that the name is supposed to designate.

In Borges's formulation, literature or, rather, writing, makes it possible to forget oneself (one's Self) and to forget one's place as well. However the Argentinean writer may define the tradition to which he says to belong, it is its disuse as knowledge that is important for Borges and where he reads a mark of innovation. For this reason, Italian themes can "belong" to the English literary tradition by way of Chaucer and Shakespeare, as the essay states, just as the French and English literary traditions may "belong" to the Argentinean tradition by way of Güiraldes. As translations, literary and artistic texts suppose an errancy into foreignness, of Self and country ("Creo que si nos abandonamos a ese sueño voluntario que se llama la creación artística, seremos argentinos y seremos, también, buenos o tolerables escritores" (EA 274) [I believe that if we abandon ourselves in the voluntary dream called artistic creation, we will be Argentine and we will be, as well, good or tolerable writers (427), translation modified]), an errancy that disarticulates the integrity of the terms sustained by the hierarchies center/margin, metropolitan/subaltern, foreign/national.

Instead of serving as an illustration or example of the story, "El escritor argentino y la tradición," therefore, puts in doubt the homology between the essay and "El aleph." If, as Piglia states, for Borges the universe can be found in the basement of a house on Garay Street, that is, in the foundational house of the Nation (Juan de Garay is the name of the founder of Buenos Aires) and that universe is the very content of Carlos Argentino Daneri's laughable poem, then the knowledge to be found in the Aleph is rejected in the story and cannot be considered the triumphant acquisition of a subaltern, South American writer. The end of the first part of the story indicates as much; it comes immediately after Borges the narrator (hereon referred to as "Borges") has "seen" the Aleph: "En la calle, en las escaleras de Constitución, en el subterráneo, me parecieron familiares todas las caras. Temí que no quedara una solo cosa capaz de sorprenderme, temí que no me abandonara jamás la impresión de volver. Felizmente, al cabo de unas noches de insomnio, me trabajó otra vez el olvido"[22] [Out in the street, on the steps of the Constitución Station, in the subway, all the faces seemed familiar. I feared that there was nothing that had the power to surprise me any more, I feared that the feeling of returning would never leave me. Happily, after a few sleepless nights, forgetting began to work on me again (284), translation modified] (A 626).

The story then does not center on how from the subaltern space occupied by an Argentinean writer he may gain access to universal knowledge, but on the need to forget that knowledge, just as at the end of the second part of the story "Borges" cannot remember the face of Beatriz. This forgetting is accompanied by the destruction of the house—its imminent destruction is the reason Carlos Argentino Daneri first contacts "Borges." Instead of allowing access and the possibility of mixing or combining elements of the various traditions that the Aleph includes, the Aleph is virtually a de-appropriating machine; knowledge is not its product for "Borges." What remains for the writer once this occurs, what does he make "use" of once he has been "unworked" by forgetting ("me trabajó otra vez el olvido")? Certainly not the contents of a national literature, however heterogeneous it may be—the destruction of the house (and one supposes of the Aleph) points in this direction.

NATIONAL MYTHS, DE-TOTALIZING TRANSLATIONS

The dis-appropriation of knowledge that the Aleph puts into effect undermines the philosophical concept of Subject, which forms the basis of all notions of representation. From his house of national being ("la casa del ser nacional") Daneri has the will to transcribe the totality of the universe into the language of his poem in order to make a name for himself, to become a famous poet. This desire of Daneri's is analogous to the Genesis story of the Tower of Babel where the tribe of the Shems also wishes to make a name for themselves by creating a universal language, which would be the only language spoken on earth. The Shems desire a unity of place (the Tower) so that they will no longer be scattered.[23]

The desire for mastery and the will to communion that the poem represents for Daneri can also be said to define the function of myth. Essentially concerned with revealing and founding, myth is a narrative of origins and a teleological representation of collective destiny.[24] As such, myth is communitarian because it seeks to represent "the unique voice of the many."[25] The jury that awards Daneri the National Prize for Literature recognizes the mythic function of his poem as the representation of the national community. Indeed, the desire for a unity of place as the locus of linguistic and communal union is evident in Daneri's poem "The Earth," where he proposes to make of the Aleph's simultaneity of time, a totalizing description of space:

Éste se proponía versificar toda la redondez del planeta; en 1941 ya había despachado una hectáreas del estado de Queensland, más de un kilómetro del curso de Ob, un gasómetro al norte de Veracruz, las principales casas de comercio de la parroquia de Concepción, la quinta de Mariana Cambaceres de Alvear en la calle Once de Setiembre, en Bel-

grano y un establecimiento de baños turcos no lejos del acreditado acu-
ario de Brighton. Me leyó ciertos laboriosos pasajes de la zona
australiana de su poema. (620)

[His goal was to versify the entire planet; by 1941 he had already completed several hectares of the state of Queensland, more than a kilometer
of the course of Ob, a gasworks north of Veracruz, the leading commer-
cial establishments in the parish of Concepción, Mariana Cambaceres
de Alvear's villa on Once de Setiembre Street in Belgrano, and a Turk-
ish bath not far from the famed Brighton aquarium. He read me certain
laborious passages from the Australian region of his poem. (277), translation modified]

Lévi-Strauss defines myth as the turning of time into space, as a
grid on which world, society, and history are conferred meanings.[26]
In effect, myth making is a putting in representation and figuring
the world; for this reason it is considered foundational, concerned
as it is with constructing and building. Myth, therefore, is a narrative that provides the ground on which to build and found the collective. And this meaning of ground and this ground of meaning is
of course what Daneri believes he has found in the basement of his
house on Garay Street. For Daneri the Aleph is the possibility of
founding a national myth. Through his experience of the Aleph
Daneri wishes to create a totalizing literature in which image and
meaning will converge and whose very language will be the revelation of truth, of the truth of his poem as representative of the national community, as in Lugones's *Odas Seculares*.

It is in his rejection of Daneri's (and Lugones's) desire to produce a literature tied to a logic of identity (the production of a national myth as the myth of the People's self-formation), that
Borges's "El Aleph" also becomes a denunciation of fascism and
of the fascist conception of art.[27] Borges's position regarding fascism was well known. In a special issue of the literary magazine
Sur published in 1940 and dedicated to an analysis of the war in
Europe, Borges condemns the Nazis and aligns himself with England and France: "Es posible que una derrota alemana sea la ruina
de Alemania; es indiscutible que su victoria sería la ruina y el envilecimiento del orbe."[28] Because of his position regarding Nazism
and its conceptions of the work of art, in the story Borges presents
the contours of an aesthetic project that interrupts the fascist desire
for myth.

This interruption comes in the form of "Borges's" experience of the Aleph, which sows confusion and forgetting on Daneri's desire for mastery. As we learn in the second part of the story, immediately after "Borges" sees the Aleph, the house/tower is destroyed, as in the Genesis story, and as the only other "witness" to the Aleph "Borges" is incapable of a successful translation; he is incapable of transmitting its Truth, as Daneri desires.

There is a gap between the time of the Aleph and the time of writing. For this reason "Borges" complains, "Arribo, ahora al inefable centro de mi relato, empieza, aquí, mi desesperación de escritor" [I come now to the ineffable center of my story; here begins my desperation as a writer" (282), translation modified] (624). The Aleph functions like what Benjamin calls a sacred text in which the letter and sense (or meaning) cannot be disassociated. Or as in Hölderlin's translation of Sophocles, according to Benjamin: "In them the harmony of the languages is so profound that sense is touched by language only the way an aeolian harp is touched by the wind . . . For this very reason Hölderlin's translations in particular are subject to the enormous danger inherent in all translations: the gates of a language thus expanded and modified may slam shut and enclose the translator with silence."[29] The Aleph thus marks the limit of Borgesian writing because it is simultaneously what cannot be translated (it thus functions like a proper, unique name) but also what requires translation, since it belongs to a common system, language.

As in "El escritor argentino y la tradición," where Borges speaks of translating Paseo Colón into the Rue de Toulon, the proper name theoretically should not be in need of translation, as it unambiguously names a concrete place or individual. However, in the essay Borges shows that writing presupposes a system of differences which puts in doubt the notion of the proper. In this way, he decomposes the unity and uniqueness of the proper name Argentina, as well as its adjectivation into literature, culture, and tradition. For the proponents of cultural nationalism such a translation would not be possible, as the nation's name, its appellation, is one and absolute. It is for this reason that Daneri believes that by writing his poem titled "La Tierra" ("The Earth"), he is, in effect, translating in a literal and original way; that is, he is writing an original, proper poem and for those same reasons, a national poem.

Closer to a Cervantes, Goethe, Shakespeare, or Hernández than to Carlos Argentino Daneri, in "El aleph" "Borges" is exposed to the anguish of the post-Babelic writer. When translating from a foreign language or into one, the writer experiences the strangeness of the language that he considers his own. Translation requires creating comparisons and resemblances where there are none. Borges states: "Todo lenguaje es un alfabeto de símbolos cuyo ejercicio presupone un pasado que los interlocutores comparten, cómo transmitir [or translate, one might say] el infinito Aleph que mi temerosa memoria apenas abarca?" (624) [Every language is an alphabet of symbols the employment of which assumes a past shared by its interlocutors. How can one transmit to others the infinite Aleph, which my timorous memory can hardly contain? (282)]. The problem that "Borges" speaks of here "exists" because the text to be translated no longer belongs to the original language or even to the language into which it will be translated. Subtracted from its "original" language it begins to inhabit an uncertain "place" and the text that we thought was original, fixed, and definitive, is in fact incomplete, unstable, full of silences and secrets, and so is the translation.[30]

The descent into the basement where the Aleph is housed does not offer, as Daneri would wish, any revelation for "Borges," no truth, no sense that could be captured through writing. Indeed, as he states in "El escritor argentino y la tradición," it is when he no longer seeks to find [encontrar] but, rather, to abandon himself that the "sense" is communicated, even though it is no longer a sense which depends on direction or final meaning. Language, "Borges" indicates, resists a total translation, even though the force of that writing is the desire for communication, a desire that is also related to the desire for Beatriz. Desire for impossible reconciliations, for fascinating and monstrous unions. Why fascinating and monstrous? Because in the Aleph "Borges" finds the very possibility of being able to say everything (the dream of every writer) but he also finds the unsayable itself—death—what cannot be articulated by language. But even given this situation, those desires of communication persist; they are not erased for being impossible or outside the reach of language.

As the second part of the story indicates (the postdata), the faint rumor of the Aleph, the narrator tells us, can still be heard in a column (the only one left standing after the destruction of the Tower?) in a republic founded by nomads. The Aleph, intimates this part of the story, still functions as a horizon, although it is now exiled, outside the West (in Cairo), outside the register of phonetic and alphabetic writing, and outside the parameters of a national territory (one supposes that a republic of nomads is an impossibility). The Aleph, that secret and conjectural object whose contents are impossible to translate, marks the limit of Borgesian writing, the failure of language, but also the possibility of writing itself. Isn't the story that we read also titled "El aleph," even though this Aleph has been un-worked by forgetting, un-constructed through the traces and rests of a total and infinite knowledge?

No language is one language, Borges indicates repeatedly; the supposed original is always already dis-articulated, exiled, exposed to an infinite errancy. As the narrator states at the end of "El inmortal" [The Immortal], the writer works with displaced and mutilated words. Translations then are fragments of fragments, and like the amphora in Benjamin's essay on translation, those fragments can never reconstruct a totality. Borges's writing thus follows the logic of the *pharmakon*, of which I spoke at the beginning of this chapter. In his writing what I said was secret or mysterious is of course language itself, a language which promises to translate the spirit of what we call *patria*, but which simultaneously frustrates all possibility of proclaiming the existence of a national literature.

"Beatriz querida, Beatriz perdida para siempre": On Death, Desire, and the Image

Write to be able to die—Die to be able to write.
—M. Blanchot, *L'espace littéraire*

The work of mourning: the opposite of dying.
—M. Blanchot, *Le pas au-delà*

If the Aleph marks the limit of Borgesian writing (as what both allows and disavows communication), its relation to death must be examined. Death as the possibility and impossibility of writing is a constant problem in Borges's texts and in "El Aleph" the implications of death's ambiguity are emphatically exposed. On one level "Borges's" yearly pilgrimages to the house on Garay Street after Beatriz Viterbo's death (according to the story she dies in 1929 and the story is dated 1941), the account of which makes up the better part of the story, points to a traditional relation between the concept of death and the possibilities it affords for narration and representation, as well as to the idea of time as progressive and chronological. In fact, the negative power of language is central to this part of the story. Following Hegel, "language, and thus humankind in general, find their truth in the finitude embodied in death, because death is the source of the negativity that separates sign from object and by making language possible makes humanity and literature possible too."[31] The narrator's work of mourning thus makes death an object that can be transcended and in turn made into a beginning, the opening onto an infinite becoming. Indeed, Beatriz Viterbo's death makes the narration of the story titled "El aleph" possible; her end is the story's beginning:

> La candente mañana de febrero en que Beatriz Viterbo murió . . . noté que las carteleras de fierro de la Plaza Constitución habían renovado no sé qué aviso de cigarrillos rubios; el hecho me dolió, pues comprendí que el incesante y vasto universo ya se apartaba de ella y que ese cambio era el primero de una serie infinita. (617)

> [On the sweltering morning in February that Beatriz Viterbo died . . . I noticed that a new advertisement for some cigarettes or other (blondes, I believe they were) had been posted on the iron billboard of the Plaza Constitución; the fact deeply grieved me, for I realized that the vast unceasing universe was already growing away from her, and that this change was but the first in an infinite series. (274)]

Although they seem to be intellectual and romantic rivals, for both "Borges" and Daneri the house is the site and possibility of representation. For Daneri the Aleph is an object which provides him with the possibility of constructing a universal and, therefore, national narrative; for "Borges" Beatriz's death is the very possibility of mourning and in so doing, narrating his desire: "muerta yo podía consagrarme a su memoria, sin esperanza, pero también sin humillación" (617) [now that she was dead, I could consecrate myself to her memory—without hope, but also without humiliation (274)].

However, "Borges's" experience of the Aleph will disturb the pacific notion of narration as the possibility of representation by pointing to writing as the impossibility of death. Indeed, it is after seeing the Aleph that the narrator reaches the ineffable center of the narrative, it is when the negative power of language breaks down:

> el problema central es irresoluble: la enumeración, siquiera parcial, de un conjunto infinito . . . Lo que vieron mis ojos fue simultáneo. Lo que

transcribiré, sucesivo, porque el lenguage lo es. Algo, sin embargo, re-
cogeré. (625)

[the central problem—the enumeration, even partial enumeration, of infinity—is irresolvable . . . What my eyes saw was simultaneous; what I
shall write, successive, because language is successive. Something of it,
though, I will collect. (282–3), translation modified.]

In this passage there is an emphatic, repetitive insistence on the
act of seeing, although the experience of the Aleph makes problematic the relation between the order of cognition and the order of representation. Prior (or outside) language, what is seen cannot be
known. That "something" which is not a thing, may be called, following Maurice Blanchot, an image:

The gaze gets taken in, absorbed by an immobile movement and a
depthless deep. What is given us by this contact at a distance is the
image, and fascination is passion for the image. What fascinates us robs
us of our power to give sense . . . It no longer reveals itself to us, and
yet it affirms itself in a presence foreign to the temporal present and
to presence in space. Separation, which was the possibility of seeing,
coagulates at the very center of the gaze into impossibility. The look
thus finds, in what makes it possible, the power that neutralizes it, neither suspending or arresting it, but on the contrary preventing it from
ever finishing, cutting it off from any beginning, making of it a neutral
directionless gleam which will not go out, yet does not clarify.[32]

Neither a sign nor a value, the image is outside the register of meaning or truth. For this reason, "seeing" the Aleph does not succeed
in making it an object; a paradoxical fact that Daneri makes clear
when he tauntingly tells "Borges," before the latter's descent into
the basement, "muy en breve podrás entablar un diálogo con *todas
las imágenes de Beatriz*" (624, emphasis in the original) [within a
very short while you will be able to begin a dialogue with *all* the
images of Beatriz (282)]. Daneri's use of the word "image" (imagen) denotes accurately that the Aleph does not belong to the order
of representation, thus marking the interruption of what constitutes
the narration of the first part of the story. If upstairs "Borges"
could only approach Beatriz's portraits (retratos), realist representations of an absence, with the Aleph "Borges" comes face to face
with the cadaver, that "reliquia atroz" [horrendous remains] that
defies representation because, properly speaking, the status of the

cadaver is neither that of an absence or a presence, but instead that of the image.

The images the Aleph exposes escape the order of representation precisely because death is not an end in the Aleph; the images are infinite, not restricted to the finite presupposed in the negative power of death. Thus, as Daneri tauntingly says, "Borges" is able to dialogue with all the images of Beatriz precisely because Beatriz is not dead enough, can never be dead enough. And because these images point to an excessiveness or alterity that cannot be accounted for, they cannot be incorporated into an economy and appropriated as knowledge.   .

In *Letras de Borges*, Sylvia Molloy notes that the ends in Borges's texts are never the end, they are "muertes desviadas" [strayed deaths], always interrupted by the work of textuality that by making them change sign, also makes them begin again, but differently.[33] Death in "El aleph" is at one level the work of the negative, as we have said, a fact which is established when the narrator states his theory of language ("el problema central es irresoluble" [the central problem is irresolvable]). Additionally, alongside a negative aspect of death inscribed in a progressive dialectic of endless becoming, there is another ambiguous idea of death in Borges, some "thing" which by its very impossibility is what precedes the end and allows the singularity of "things" to appear, as it were, pre-objectively.

This latter notion of death is what makes writing possible but can never appear as such; it is what Borges calls in "La muralla y los libros" [The Wall and the Book] "la inminencia de una revelación que no se produce"[34] [the imminence of a revelation that is never produced (346), translation modified]. Therefore, as in Beatriz's image, it is more dying than death itself that we read in Borges, like in "El muerto" [The Dead Man] when the death of Otálora is only the redundant end of the one which preceded it: "porque ya lo daban por muerto, porque para Bandeira ya estaba muerto. Suárez, casi con desdén, hace fuego"[35] [because he was already as good as dead, because for Bandeira he was already dead Suárez fires, almost with a sneer (200), translation modified].

The complicated temporality of dying implies that death can never be made present. Otálora's "final" end is only the repetition of a past that was never present and thus complicates the future that can never be made present either. It is impossible to control death in Borges's texts, impossible to make it one's work. It is never the completion of a destiny, the end of a life's work. In fact, because my death cannot be experienced as such (precisely because I can never say "I am dead"), death is never mine to have; the work of the negative, as well as all notions of appropriation thus become impossible. Dying undoes any notion of mastery, any idea of a self-present subject. I cannot control what always either precedes me or is outside my grasp (or experience) and, for this reason, I am unable to produce a discourse on this "excess," which is irreducible to a magisterial position.

One could say that Daneri's fear of the destruction of the house and, therefore, of the Aleph, is the fear of death itself. His wish to make a name for himself, to become a famous poet is to have his name somehow survive him. What Daneri does not realize is that his name in life already marks his death and opens him to an alterity, a de-appropriation for which he cannot account. Daneri wants to circumvent the law of translation, he wants to be first and thinks that the Aleph will allow him to do just that.

"Borges's" experience of the Aleph presents an alternative to Daneri's aesthetics:

vi un adorado monumento en la Chacarita, vi la reliquia atroz de lo que deliciosamente había sido Beatriz Viterbo, vi la circulación de mi oscura sangre, vi el engranaje del amor y la modificación de la muerte . . . vi mi cara y mis vísceras, *vi tu cara* y sentí vértigo y lloré, porque mis ojos habían visto ese objeto secreto y conjetural, cuyo nombre usurpan los hombres, pero que ningún hombre ha mirado: el inconcebible universo. (626, my emphasis)

[I saw a beloved monument in Chacarita, saw the horrendous remains of what had once, deliciously, been Beatriz Viterbo, saw the circulation of my dark blood, saw the coils and springs of love and the alteration of death . . . saw my face and my viscera, saw *your* face and I felt dizzy and wept, because my eyes had seen that secret and conjectural object whose name has been usurped by men but which no man has ever looked upon: the inconceivable universe. (283–4), emphasis mine, translation modified]

The list of things that "Borges" sees in the Aleph is part of a necessarily incomplete narrative that tries to capture the simultaneity of the inconceivable universe. In this sense the Aleph could be said to be the reverse of Borges's Chinese Encyclopedia that Michele Foucault analyzes in *The Order of Things*.[36] For Foucault the notion of order is suspended in the heteroclite rendering of the encyclopedia by the removal of the grounds on which that order is founded. But, if the encyclopedia interrupts the notion of a common locus, the Aleph would posit the possibility of restituting the order of things, of making word and thing coincide. The repetitive use of the word "vi" (I saw) makes the cognitive rendering of a self-present Subject the guarantor of such coincidence.

Indeed, in the basement of the house on Garay Street, there is nothing to be found, nothing to be discovered, but the self-present truth that, like the purloined letter, is exhibited for anyone to see.[37] And yet, it is precisely the mention of a certain "presence" ("tu cara" [your face]) that interrupts the narration of things seen; an interruption followed by vertigo and tears, "porque mis ojos habían visto ese objeto secreto y conjetural, cuyo nombre usurpan los hombres, pero que ningún hombre ha mirado: el inconcebible universo" (626) [because my eyes had seen that secret and conjectural object whose name has been usurped by men but which no man has ever looked upon: the inconceivable universe (284)].

What is that face that interrupts the flow of cognition and inscribes an inhuman or, perhaps, "divine" presence? I say inhuman or divine precisely because "Borges" takes such care in informing us that no man ("ningún hombre") had seen it before. The interruption of the list comes precisely because of an ineffable *prosopopeia*: the "tu cara" that gives a face to what is nonexistent, making the invisible, visible.[38] This prosopopeic moment marks a turning point in the story. As we will see, the crisis in language that prosopopeia exposes allows for the subsequent formulation of a poetics. This crisis will also complicate the notions of referentiality and signification, the here and now of which the story's epigraph from *Leviathan* speaks.

Prosopopeia is a trope of apostrophe, of address; it thus figures the reader and the act of reading. How does "tu cara" complicate these two figures? A prosopopeic figure is catachrestic; "tu cara" points to what does not exist except at the moment of being named. As we saw in the analysis of Martínez Estrada in chapter 2, catachresis (as in the example "face of a mountain") has no proper existence as a signifier, but comes into being in the process of signification. This is an important point because as Paul DeMan shows, a referent can only be certain inasmuch as it is open to phenomenalization: "the phenomenal and sensory properties of the signifier have to serve as guarantors for the certain existence of the signified and, ultimately, of the referent."[39]

Indeed, in the part of Borges's list we are here reading, the signifiers are presented in phenomenological terms: "vi un adorado monumento en la Chacarita, vi la reliquia atroz de lo que deliciosamente había sido Beatriz Viterbo, vi la circulación de mi oscura sangre, vi el engranaje del amor y la modificación de la muerte . . . vi mi cara y mis vísceras." (626) [I saw a beloved monument in Chacarita, saw the horrendous remains of what had once, deliciously, been Beatriz Viterbo, saw the circulation of my dark blood, saw the coils and springs of love and the alteration of death . . . saw my face and my viscera" (283–84)]. The senses, and especially self-consciousness, are the material signs of an event (the passage of time, death) that is suddenly interrupted by the prosopopeic "tu cara," which cannot be accounted for by any prior sensory experience.

Prosopopeia thus undoes the relation between reference and signification. Following Hegel, if consciousness (I see, I hear, I think) is supposed to guarantee its relation to time, space, and self, prosopopeia as catachresis undoes this relation. The narrator's experience of the Aleph, then, gives credence to the epigraph from *Leviathan* at the beginning of the story:

> But they will teach us that Eternity is the Standing still of the Present Time, a Nunc-stans (as the Schools call it); which neither they, nor anyone else understand, no more than they would a Hic-stans for an Infinite greatness of Place. *Leviathan*, IV, 46. (617)

The infinite universe that is the Aleph is not able to secure the *hic* and *nunc* of consciousness, the coincidence between cognition and signification. For this reason, the Aleph becomes a false Aleph in the postdata, a mis-understanding, one of the many other Alephs that are said to exist; a situation that puts into question the referentiality presupposed by the order of cognition. That is, how can a false Aleph produce an original literature?[40]

The Aleph destroys all notions of referentiality based on a prior definition of culture; the here and now is inscribed not as a sign but, rather, as what constantly interrupts all figurality and all reference. In this sense, as we stated at the beginning of this chapter, Borges's texts point to the impossibility of translation if by such a concept we understand the possibility of a totalizing notion of knowledge. The Aleph destroys the notion of translation as metaphor, as the transference, without loss, of one system into another.

If for Daneri the Aleph is the very ground on which to found a national literature, for "Borges" the Aleph exposes language to an alterity it cannot master or even know. And it is important that it is precisely when "Borges" is on the ground, when he is literally on the ground of the house on Garay Street, that the ground is no longer under him. Paradoxically, the infinite Aleph exposes the impossibility of a totalizing notion of literature: an impossibility that is a constitutive part of that very supposed totality.

The experience of the Aleph "shows" that the writer's "starting point" is not the closure of a system, a tradition, or a historical period: a post (modern or otherwise) supposed to mark the closure of metaphysics, as if such a tradition were a thing of the past and not what is exposed in the very act of writing as the impossibility of writing itself.[41] It is precisely at this point, if it can be so-called, where the uncanny aspect of Borges's writing is most extreme, given that it cannot be identified as a space outside or beyond metaphysics, but rather as what interrupts the totalizing impulse of metaphysics in its very search for plenitude. The interruption lies in writing's inability to be totally incorporated into a metaphysical economy, thus allowing for an unrepresentable opening (which cannot be thought under the logic of recuperation) to be imagined: for that which is to come.

The economy of loss, end, and mourning is problematized by the question of the gifts in the story. In fact, the narrator's yearly visits to the house on Garay Street have the flavor of celebrating a national holiday, a fact which is marked by the meager and autochthonous gifts (the "alfajor," the cheap, national cognac disdained by Daneri) that the narrator brings on the date that he considers to have been Beatriz's birthday: "Consideré que el treinta de abril era su cumpleaños." (617) [I considered that the thirtieth of April was her birthday], although the wording suggests that the date is uncertain or arbitrary.

If gifts can be said to involve both the giver and the receiver in a law and an economy of indebtedness, it is because gift giving is a form of exchange; it enacts a scene of obligation to follow the law and return the gift made.[42] However, if the gift were simply part of an economy of exchange that supposed a reciprocal and symmetrical system of restitution, the gift could not even be considered a problem given that, strictly speaking, if there is a gift there is no gift since the law of exchange is already inscribed in its economy, thus making impossible the singular and free character of the gift. For this reason, if there is a gift it must pass through an economy that exceeds the reciprocity of exchange.

The importance of gift giving in "El aleph" is that exchange is directly connected to the problem of referentiality and, therefore, to metaphor and translation. Surprisingly, Daneri announces the Aleph's possibility of circumventing the law of gift. It is right after "Borges" "sees" the Aleph: "no me pagarás en un siglo esta revelación" (626) [you will not repay me for this revelation in a century]. The malicious irony of his remark is that the "revelation" "Borges" receives as a gift (the image of the incestuous letters written by Beatriz to her cousin Daneri) is precisely what prohibits its exchange; the image (the content of the revelation) exposes the impossibility of Beatriz becoming an object of exchange, given that incest defies the law of exchange. Further, the "revelation" of the Aleph will not be repaid even in a century, according to Daneri, because the Aleph is infinite and not exposed to the subject-object duality on which the negative aspect of language is based. As we have seen, the Aleph enacts a complicated temporality in which the end is not the end and the gift is not properly a gift. And, if the Aleph circumvents the law of exchange, then one can say that it also circumvents the notion of transference (one thing for another) and, therefore, of translation.

At the beginning of this chapter I said that for Borges translation was an impossibility. Even though translation is a constant preoccupation in his texts, its failure is always assumed and even assured. In fact, by putting in question the notion of exchange, which implies death, by complicating the phenomenal and the cognitive apprehension of an object as the means of attaining knowledge, by making referentiality a problem and not a given, Borges in "El aleph" presents a form of writing that responds to what cannot be written. The aleph is the writer's exposure to what is not within the realm of comparison, to what cannot be translated, exchanged or even mourned. It is the event of language itself that marks a singular-plural experience of being in common.

Concluding Remarks

> Comunidad: disfrutada por varios sin pertencer a ninguno en particular.
>
> [Community: enjoyed by many without belonging to any one in particular].
>
> —*Diccionario de la Real Academia Española*
> [*Dictionary of the Spanish Royal Academy*]

IN "EL ALEPH" BORGES PRESENTED THE NEED TO INTERRUPT THE notion of an immanent (totalizing) community by showing the limits of those elements that inscribe the literary within an economy that, throughout the preceding chapters, I have called the quest of identity. Published more than twenty years later, Borges's "El congreso" ["The Congress"] (1975) rewrites the earlier story[1] and in so doing presents a notion of community "enacted" in its very dissolution and indefinition, a community of dissensus, to borrow a phrase from Giogio Agamben.[2]

"El congreso" relates the plans of a "secret society" to create a "Congreso del Mundo" [Congress of the World] that "representaría a todos los hombres de todas las naciones" [would represent all people of all nations].[3] Under the leadership of a wealthy land-owner, the society meets weekly in order to plan the future founding of the congress that is to take place in four years. Some members, including the narrator, are sent on research trips in order to investigate the language and books that will best represent the world.

The question of representation and its multiple meanings (in politics, as well as in art and philosophy) is therefore the story's central focus, developed on separate but parallel levels. On one level is the self-questioning of the narrator's ability to represent the plans of the society. He feels inadequate and unequal to the job assigned to him, given his lack of experience in literary endeavors; his uncertainty also stems from the fact that he is giving testimony of a sworn secret. On another level, the story relates the problems in-

120

volved in the political forms of representation of the future congress:

> Twirl, cuya inteligencia era lúcida, observó que el Congreso presuponía un problema de índole filosófica. Planear una asamblea que representara a todos los hombres era como fijar el número exacto de los arquetipos platónicos, enigma que ha atareado durante siglos la perplejidad de los pensadores. Sugirió que, sin ir más lejos, don Alejandro Glencoe podía representar a los hacendados, pero también a los orientales y también a los grandes precursores y también a los hombres de barba roja y a los que están sentados en un sillón. Nora Erfjord era noruega. ¿Representaría a las secretarias, a las noruegas o simplemente a todas las mujeres hermosas? ¿Bastaba un ingeniero para representar a todos los ingenieros, incluso los de Nueva Zelandia? (C 24).

> [Twirl, a man of lucid intelligence, remarked that the Congress presented a problem of a philosophical nature. Designing a body of men and women that would represent all humanity was akin to fixing the exact number of Platonic archetypes, an enigma that has engaged the perplexity of philosophers for centuries. He suggested, therefore that (to take but one example) don Alejandro Glencoe might represent ranchers, but also Uruguayans, as well as founding fathers and red-bearded men and men sitting in armchairs. Nora Erfjord was Norwegian. Would she represent secretaries, Norwegians, or simply all the beautiful women? Was one engineer sufficient to represent all engineers, even engineers from New Zealand? (426–27)]

Borges poses a problem that the decline of the nation as the guarantor of collective as well as personal identity presents. If the "I" has always been defined in terms of collective "we" and that "we" does not have a stable and grounded referent, then how should identity and its necessary representation be thought? In other words, if no archetype or essential model can be established to serve as the ground of representation, then the notion of mediation, of that which would serve as the conduit between model and copy is also done away with.

As in many of Borges's texts where lists appear, there is no common ground that might unify the heteroclite elements comprising the list. In the case of Glencoe, for example, if he can be said to be the representative of class, nation, age, or of certain physical attributes, the inclusion of "those who are seated on a couch" undoes, by its very absurdity, the pertinence that all the other traditional categories of representation seemed to hold.

Given that in the story the Congreso del Mundo pretends to "represent all people of all nations" and the difficulties and impossibilities of such a representation are also demonstrated, is "El congreso" proposing that a non-identifiable and non-identical community be represented? Not if by representation we understand fixing, stabilizing, or defining what cannot or refuses to be so understood. In "El aleph," as we saw in chapter 4, Borges removes the grounds on which the order of representation is founded; he presents a poetics of writing that is not tied to any single foundation or identity, whether that foundation or identity is defined in national, linguistic, economic, or literary terms. In "El congreso" he presents the possibility of thinking community "starting" from the removal of those grounds.

Even though two of its members are sent to research the language which should be the official language of the "Congreso del Mundo," that language is never found; the location which is to serve as its headquarters (somewhere between Uruguay and Brazil) is sold; the library, which was to contain all the books in the world and was housed in the basement of the president's house, is destroyed.

There is no one unifying element, then, capable of holding the congress together as one, nor is it possible to locate it within any modern notion of an imagined community. The moment that was to mark its foundation becomes the end of "founding" and the "beginning" of an always already begun world: "la empresa que hemos acometido es tan vasta que abarca . . . el mundo entero . . . El Congreso del Mundo comenzó con el primer instante del mundo y proseguirá cuando seamos polvo [The task we have undertaken is so vast that it embraces . . . the entire world . . . The Congress of the World began the instant the world itself began, and it will go on when we are dust (434)] (31). The congress itself cannot be represented because as its "president" states: "No hay un lugar en que no esté" [There is no place it is not (434)] (31). This is an enigmatic and ambiguous pronouncement given that, depending on the emphasis, it could mean both that the congress is nowhere and everywhere, and, of course, that is precisely the point.

The type of community that the congress presupposes is a non-identifiable and un-representable community, which, nevertheless, lives on, survives in the narrator's re-presentation: "Sin mayor esperanza, he buscado a lo largo de los años el sabor de esa noche; alguna vez creí recuperarla en la música, en el amor, en la incierta memoria, pero no ha vuelto, salvo una sola madrugada en un sueño" (32) [With no great hope, through all these years I have sought the savor of that night; once in a great while I have thought I caught a snatch of it in a song, in lovemaking, in uncertain memory, but it has never fully come back to me save once, one early morning, in a dream (436)]. However, this re-presentation "belongs" to the unconscious and, therefore, not to the order of the phenomenal: to what can be apprehended in a cognitive manner as an object of representation.

In Borges, community appears in its disappearance; it is an unavowable community that leaves traces of its existence in the singular experience of the narrator, even if those traces, much as ruins in Benjamin, cannot be made into a figure or reach completed form.[4] In my analysis of Borges in chapter 4, I said that a central problematic for this writer was to write in a language which is both shared and yet untranslatable, given that Borges rejects the notion of a linguistic community capable of assuring the transparent transmission of sense. In "El congreso" Borges again repeats, with certain variations, what was first stated in "El aleph": "Las palabras son símbolos que postulan una memoria compartida" (31) [Words are symbols that posit a shared memory (435)]. Yet the moment of community that marks the existence of the congress itself cannot be shared: "La que ahora quiero historiar es mía solamente; quienes la compartieron han muerto" (31) [The memory I want to set down for posterity now is mine alone; those who shared it have all died (435)]. Language is what makes community possible and impossible in Borges; the narrator must resort, as we have already seen, to the traces of an experience which "happened" in a dream.

This explains why the narration of the congress is itself deficient and highlights the deficiencies of narration. Narration has been considered traditionally as the relation of events containing a beginning, middle, and end (much like the economy of travel I have discussed throughout *Being in Common*), as well as the conduit through which one accedes to the knowledge of an object.[5] Narration is, therefore, the privileged form for expressing the nation, as Anderson and Bhabha demonstrate so well, since it gives a form and a body to the collective and provides the ground of its common being. Narration makes the nation an object of knowledge. In Borges's story, by contrast, the failure to narrate the congress is testament to nothing else than the impossibility of narration. Borges exposes the impossibility of writing "starting" from a notion of identity, foundational or otherwise, or from a masterful self-conscious subject. For this reason, "El congreso" writes community as the unrepresentable and unlocalizable gap that escapes ends and means rationality, as well as the limits of already sedimented forms. Borges thus ungrounds the political in writing and makes this very ungrounding our being in common.[6]

Reading is a central problematic throughout *Being in Common* and one could say that Borges takes to its limits the ways in which writing always exceeds the theories that are supposed to explain, interpret, apprehend, and, therefore, keep that writing in check. As we also saw in our analyses of texts by Carpentier, Martínez Estrada, and Paz in the preceding chapters, writing is either insufficient or excessive to the task it must fulfill. Whether a literary or cultural text is studied as an example, model or representation, that is, as an "object" of study, the writers here indicate that the text will never "live up to" the expectations of the critic or even, as in the case of Carpentier, to those of the writer himself.

If, as I have indicated, the quest of identity is one of the most persistent paradigms of cultural and critical production in Latin American texts, then the concept of travel, the aporias of translation, the problematic status of the image, and the ambiguous stance of the example, remind us in diverse and often ambiguous or contradictory ways, that the reader's task, if there is one, is to remain vigilant to re-grounding and, therefore re-inscribing those very concepts that the texts constantly dismantle. Reading thus becomes an ungrounded act, open to an unending wandering which, nevertheless, allows the singularity of literary texts to be exposed.

Notes

INTRODUCTION

1. Carlos Alonso, *The Spanish American Regional Novel: Modernity and Autochthony* (Cambridge: Cambridge University Press, 1990), 14.

2. Ibid.

3. Alberto Moreiras, "Pastiche Identity, and Allegory of Allegory," in *Latin American Identity and Constructions of Difference*, ed. Amaryll Chanady (Minneapolis: University of Minnesota Press, 1993). Moreiras reads the identity problematic as an ideology of containment. See also Josefina Ludmer, *El género gauchesco: Un tratado sobre la patria* (Buenos Aires: Sudamericana, 1988).

4. Martin S. Stabb, *In Quest of Identity: Patterns in the Spanish American Essay of Ideas, 1890–1960* (Chapel Hill: University of North Carolina Press, 1967), 220.

5. Djelal Kadir, *Questing Fictions: Latin America's Family Romance* (Minneapolis: University of Minnesota Press, 1986), 5.

6. Ibid.

7. Georges Van Den Abbeele's *Travel as Metaphor: From Montaigne to Rousseau* (Minneapolis: University of Minnesota Press, 1992) provides the model for the economy of travel throughout *Being in Common*.

8. This temporal disjunction is discussed by Alonso, *Spanish American Regional Novel*, 11, as well as by Homi Bhabha, "DissemiNation: Time, Narrative, and the Margins of the Modern Nation," in *Nation and Narration*, ed. Homi Bhabha (London: Routledge, 1990). Alonso provides a more detailed account of Spanish America's rhetoric of temporality in his recent *The Burden of Modernity: The Rhetoric of Cultural Discourse in Spanish America* (Oxford: Oxford University Press, 1998).

9. Slavoj Žižek, *For They Know Not What They Do: Enjoyment as a Political Factor* (London: Verso, 1991), 20. Similar formulations, from different theoretical perspectives, can be found in Ernesto Laclau, "Universalism, Particularism and the Question of Identity" in *Emancipation(s)* (London: Verso, 1996) and Jacques Derrida, *The Other Heading: Reflections on Today's Europe* (Bloomington: Indiana University Press, 1992). For these philosophers the constitutive aporias in the concept allow for thinking democratic politics at present.

10. See Paul De Man, "Literary History and Literary Modernity" in *Blindness and Insight: Essays in the Rhetoric of Contemporary Criticism* (Minneapolis: University of Minnesota Press, 1983).

11. When I say that the quest paradigm is a staple in Latin American literary, cultural, and critical discourse, I mean that the quest of identity is a recurring paradigm in the writing and reading of Latin American texts. I do not mean that all

125

texts are and should be read this way, but rather that the very recurrence of this paradigm must be examined. In addition to the texts by Stabb and Kadir already mentioned, which span a twenty year period, other critical texts that foreground the quest paradigm are Roberto González Echevarría, *Alejo Carpentier: The Pilgrim at Home*; Carlos Alonso, *The Spanish American Regional Novel*; Alberto Moreiras, "Pastiche Identity and Allegory of Allegory"; Mary Louise Pratt, *Imperial Eyes: Travel Writing and Transculturation;* and Adolfo Prieto, *Los viajeros ingleses y la emergencia de la literatura argentina.*

12. Roberto González Echevarría, *The Voice of the Masters: Writing and Authority in Modern Latin American Literature* (Austin: University of Texas Press, 1985), 8–9, 40.

13. D. F. Sarmiento, *Facundo o civilización y barbarie en las pampas argentinas* (Buenos Aires: CEAL, 1979), 26.

14. Benedict Anderson, *Imagined Communities: Reflections on the Origin and Spread of Nationalism* (London: Verso, 1983).

15. See note 9 for some of the recent studies to which I am referring. See also Jean-Luc Nancy, *The Inoperative Community* (Minneapolis: University of Minnesota Press, 1991) and Jacques Rancière, *Dis-agreement: Politics and Philosophy* (Minneapolis: University of Minnesota Press, 1999).

16. Georges Van Den Abbeele, introduction to *Community at Loose Ends*, ed. Miami Theory Collective (Minneapolis: University of Minnesota Press, 1991), xii.

17. See Edward Said, *Culture and Imperialism* (New York: Alfred A. Knopf, 1993) and Bhabha, who both criticize Anderson's historical "time-line." Another important component that is missing from Anderson's schema is the relation between imagination and the unconscious. Imagination for Anderson always appears to be conscious and willed.

18. Bhabha, *Nation and Narration*, 299.

19. Aris Fioretos, "Contraction (Benjamin, Reading, History)," *MLN* 110 (1995): 564. Another difference is that if for Benjamin *jetzseit* is the temporality of the revolutionary classes or the revolution per se, for Bhabha it is the temporality of the discourse of the minority or the oppressed.

20. Ibid, 565.

21. Anderson, *Imagined Communities*, 205.

22. Critics have recently maintained that notions of unrepresentability are regressive precisely because they reject the self-representation of the minority and hence advocate that the structures of power remain intact. Benjamin's *jetzseit* forms part of a tradition of thought seeking to permanently destabilize structures of power without succumbing to a negative epistemology, which exhibits a resistance to those structures of power, but at the risk of keeping them intact.

23. The outlines of the New French Studies and the New American Studies in the context of globalization or transnational production are found in Emily Apter, *Continental Drift: From National Characters to Virtual Subjects* (Chicago: University of Chicago Press, 1999); John Carlos Rowe, ed., *Post-Nationalist American Studies* (Berkeley: University of California Press, 2000); and Donald Pease, ed., *National Identities and Post-Nationalist Narratives* (Durham: Duke University Press, 1994). Julia Kristeva explores a psychoanalytic reading of postnational belonging in *Strangers to Ourselves* (New York: Columbia University Press, 1991) and *Nations Without Nationalism* (New York: Columbia University Press, 1993).

24. Donald E. Pease, "National Narratives, Postnational Narration," *Modern Fiction Studies* 43, no. 1 (1997): 7–8.

25. Ibid, 2, my emphasis.

26. Indicative of this problem is the title of George Sanchez's contribution to Rowe's *Post-Nationalist American Studies*, "Creating The Multicultural Nation: Adventures in Post-Nationalist American Studies in the 1990's."

27. Jacques Rancière, *Dis-agreement: Politics and Philosophy* (Minneapolis: University of Minnesota Press, 1999), 28.

28. See note 9 for some of the political thinkers and philosophers to whom I am referring. Rancière provides a definition of political subjectification: "Politics is a matter of . . . modes of subjectification, . . . the production through a series of actions of a body and a capacity for enunciation not previously identifiable within a given field of experience," 35.

29. Jean-Luc Nancy uses the term being-in-common in *The Inoperative Community*.

30. Phillipe Van Haute, "Law, Guilt and Subjectivity: Reflection on Freud, Nancy and Derrida," in *Deconstructive Subjectivities*, ed. S. Critchley and P. Dews (Albany: SUNY Press, 1996), discusses the implications of Nancy's formulation "You a(nd)re (wholly other than) me" in *The Inoperative Community*.

31. Quoted in David Panagia, "Ceci n'est pas un argument: An Introduction to the Ten Theses" in *Theory & Event* 5, no. 3: 2.

32. For a history of the term "ser nacional," especially as it was developed in the Latin American essay, see Stabb; González Echevarría; Jaime Rest, *El cuarto en el recoveco* (Buenos Aires: Centro Editor, 1982); Medardo Vitier, *Del ensayismo americano* (Mexico: FCE, 1945); Robert Mead, *Breve historia del ensayo en la América Hispana* (Mexico: DeAndrea, 1956); and Pedro Henríquez Ureña, *Las corrientes literarias en la América Hispana* (Mexico: FCE, 1954).

33. In Argentina there is a long tradition of the individual (almost always a male subject) who "represents" the nation. See Alberto Gerchunoff, *El hombre que habló en la Sorbona*; Alberto Laplace, *El hombre que tuvo una idea*; Méndez Calzada, *El hombre que silba y aplaude*; José León Pagano, *El hombre que volvió a la vida*; A. Cancela, *El hombre que camina y tropieza*; and Roberto Arlt, *El hombre de las ciencias ocultas*. See also David Viñas, *Literatura argentina y política. De Lugones a Walsh* (Buenos Aires: Ed. Sudamericana, 1996), especially chapter 7: "Martínez Estrada, de Radiografía de la pampa hacia el Caribe." The role of gender in the consolidation of national identities in Latin America is explored in Doris Meyer, ed. *Reinterpreting the Spanish American Essay: Women's Writing of the 19th and 20th Centuries* (Austin: University of Texas Press, 1995). For a study of the definition of gender roles in metaphysical theories of community, see Luce Irigaray, "The Eternal Irony of the Community," in *Speculum of the Other Woman* (Ithaca: Cornell University Press, 1985).

34. Quoted in Angel Rama, *Transculturación narrativa en América Latina* (México: Siglo XXI, 1982), 20.

35. Julio Ramos, *Desencuentros de la modernidad en América Latina: Literatura y política en el siglo XIX* (Mexico: FCE, 1989), 16.

36. Jorge Luis Borges, "El idioma de los argentinos," in *El idioma de los argentinos*. (Buenos Aires: Seix Barral, 1994), 141.

37. Andrés Bello, "Gramática castellana," in *Obras Completas* (Caracas, 1951), 321, quoted in Ramos.

38. See Maurice Blanchot, *The Unavowable Community*, trans. Pierre Joris (New York: Station Hill Press, 1988).

39. Jean Franco, "The Nation as Imagined Community," in *The New Historicism*, ed. H. Aram Veeser (New York: Routledge, 1989), 204–12.

40. Ernesto Laclau, "Introduction," in *The Making of Political Identities* (London: Verso, 1994), 1. See also Jean-François Lyotard, *The Postmodern Condition: A Report on Knowledge* (Minneapolis: University of Minnesota Press, 1984).

CHAPTER 1

WRITING PLACE NAMES: TRAVEL AND THEORY IN
ALEJO CARPENTIER'S *LOS PASOS PERDIDOS*

1. Kadir's *Questing Fictions* follows this same schema. For a critique of the discovery and conquest of America as master narrative, see Román de la Campa, *Latin Americanism* (Minneapolis: University of Minnesota Press, 1999).

2. Alejo Carpentier, "Lo barroco y lo real maravilloso," in *Razón de ser, Ensayos* (Mexico: Siglo XXI, 1990), 192. All translations are my own.

3. Severo Sarduy takes up the political dimension of the baroque in *Ensayos generales sobre el barroco* (Mexico: Siglo XXI, 1987) and in "Barroco y neobarroco," in *América Latina en su literatura*, ed. C. Fernández Moreno (Mexico: Siglo XXI, 1972). See also Irlemar Chiampi, *Barroco y modernidad* (Mexico: FCE, 2000).

4. Alejo Carpentier, *El reino de este mundo*, vol. 2, *Obras Completas* (Mexico: Siglo XXI, 1997), 17.

5. On Carpentier's intellectual trajectory, including his relation to the surrealist movement, see Roberto González Echevarría, *Alejo Carpentier: The Pilgrim at Home* (Ithaca: Cornell University Press, 1990).

6. For Carpentier's views on the decadence of Europe and the promise of America, especially in the 1940s, as well as contemporary intellectuals' projects for a properly American expression, see chapters 2 and 3 of González Echevarría, *The Pilgrim at Home*. See also the narrator's condemnation of European fascism in *Los pasos perdidos*.

7. González Echevarría states: "The transition from the theories of "marvelous American reality" to *The Lost Steps* could not be more telling. Faced with the problem, implied by his theory, of being unable to establish a dialogue with his culture that does not at the same time reify that culture, being unable to be autochthonous at the moment of writing, Carpentier's only possibility is to turn himself into the object, unfolding and fragmenting the self of his prologue—interrogating his own mask," *The Pilgrim at Home*, 154.

8. This point is made by González Echevarría, *The Pilgrim at Home*; Gustavo Pérez Firmat, "El lenguaje secreto de *Los pasos perdidos*," *MLN* 99 (1984): 342–57; and S. Colás, "'Dangerous Southern Islands': Modern Aesthetics as Anaesthetics in Carpentier's *The Lost Steps* and Borges's 'The South,'" in *Modernism and its Margins: Reinscribing Cultural Modernity from Spain and Latin America*, ed. A. Geist and J. Monleón (New York: Garland, 1999).

9. See Paul De Man, "The Rhetoric of Blindness," in *Blindness and Insight* (Minneapolis: University of Minnesota Press, 1983).

10. Alejo Carpentier, *Los pasos perdidos*, vol. 2, *Obras Completas* (Mexico: Siglo XXI, 1997), 145. Further references to this text are noted parenthetically as PP.

11. Theodor Adorno and Max Horkheimer, *The Dialectic of the Enlightenment* (New York: Continuum, 1988), study Homer's Odysseus as the embodiment of the dialectic of the enlightenment. See Excursus I: "Odysseus or Myth and Enlightenment."

12. Critics often read Rosario as the patron saint of Latin America, the figure of the mother and the exotic Other. For the role of Rosario in issues related to gender and sexuality, see González Echevarría, *The Pilgrim at Home* and Mark Millington, "Gender Monologue in Carpentier's *Los pasos perdidos*," *MLN* 111 (1996): 346–67.

13. What Penelope desires is a properly idiomatic sign: unique, unmediated, and private, a sign that is not open to interpretation, substitution, reproduction, or imitation. Such a sign, of course would no longer be a sign as such. See Michael Nass, "Stumping the Sun: Toward a Postmetaphorics," in *Cultural Semiosis: Tracing the Signifier*, ed. Hugh Silverman (New York: Routledge, 1998).

14. A similar problem of identification is one of the many links between *The Lost Steps* and José Eustasio Rivera's *La vorágine*. I thank Sylvia Molloy and her students in her Spring 1999 seminar on travel literature in Latin America for calling my attention to the many connections between the two texts, as well as for a stimulating discussion.

15. In *Structural Anthropology* Lévi-Strauss notes, "Anthropology aims to be a semiological science, and takes as guiding principle that of meaning," quoted in Mercedes López-Baralt, "Los pasos encontrados de Levi-Strauss y Alejo Carpentier: literatura y antropología en el siglo veinte," *Revista del Centro de Estudios Avanzados de Puerto Rico y el Caribe* 7 (Jul.–Dec. 1988): 82. Clearly, Carpentier espouses a similar notion of praxis: "nuestro deber es el de revelar este mundo, debemos mostrar, interpretar las cosas nuestras" in "Lo barroco y lo real maravilloso," 190.

16. Mary Louise Pratt, *Imperial Eyes: Travel Writing and Transculturation* (London: Routledge, 1992), 67, 196.

17. Gonzalez Echevarría's reading of *The Lost Steps* as the *arché* of future fictions, such as Gabriel García Márquez's *One Hundred Years of Solitude*, would be one example.

18. For a detailed discussion of the scopic regime in Western thought and its critique, see Martin Jay, *Downcast Eyes* (Berkeley: University of California Press, 1994).

19. The avatars of the dual movement of the concept of mimesis span from Plato and Aristotle to the more recent writings of T. Adorno, G. Bataille, R. Girard and G. Deleuze.

20. Eduardo González, *Alejo Carpentier: el tiempo del hombre* (Caracas: Monte Avila, 1978) and González Echevarría both noted the play of mirrors in this section of the novel.

21. See Karen Taylor, "La creación musical en *Los pasos perdidos*," *Nueva Revista de Filología Hispánica*, 26 (1977), 141–53, for the importance of music in Carpentier's texts.

22. See Carpentier's *Ese Musico que Llevo Dentro 1 y 2*, vol. 10 y 11, *Obras Completas* (Mexico: Siglo XXI, 1987), especially "El adivino de aldea," 274–76 and "Una página de Rousseau," 601–2.

23. The narrator's interest in utilizing Shelley's text as a model for the Treno may also be related to Shelley's aesthetics concerning the natural sign. In "The Semiotic Desire for the Natural Sign: Poetic Uses and Political Abuses," in *The States of Theory*, ed. D. Carroll (Stanford: Stanford University Press, 1990), Murray Krieger notes that "Shelley also privileges lyric poetry among the arts because of its 'natural' relation to its author as an immediately expressive vehicle for his internality," 240.

24. See Homer, *The Odyssey*, Book 11 (Cambridge: Harvard University Press, 1995), 401–47.

25. Van Den Abbeele, *Travel as Metaphor*, 24.

26. See Dean MacCannell, *The Tourist: A New Theory of the Leisure Class* (New York: Schocken Books, 1976).

27. Chiampi, *Barroco*, 108.

28. Kadir makes a similar point regarding the epilogue to *El reino de este mundo* in *Questing Fictions*.

CHAPTER 2
IMAGE, HISTORY, TRADITION: EZEQUIEL
MARTÍNEZ ESTRADA'S ALTER-NATIONS

1. In *La cabeza de Goliat* the terms of the paradigm that Sarmiento had utilized to "read" the nation are inverted. The city occupies the place of barbarism because it was built over the "pampas" that never disappeared completely, as Sarmiento would have desired.

2. Beatriz Sarlo, *Una modernidad periférica: Buenos Aires, 1920 y 1930* (Buenos Aires: Nueva Visión, 1988).

3. Ezequiel Martínez Estrada, *Radiografía de la pampa* (Buenos Aires: Losada, 1976), 344. Further references to this texts are noted parenthetically as RP. All translations are my own.

4. Both Sarlo and Graciela Montaldo, *De pronto, el campo. Literatura argentina y tradición rural* (Rosario: Beatriz Viterbo Editora, 1993) make this point. Other critics who in the 1950s and 1960s develop their own versions of Argentinean culture based on Martínez Estrada's critique of Argentinean society are David Viñas, Juan José Sebreli, Juan José Hernández Arregui, and Arturo Jauretche.

5. In a letter to his close friend Horacio Quiroga, Martínez Estrada explains why he decided not to publish again after *Radiografía de la pampa*. See Carlos Adam, *Bibliografía y documentos de Ezequiel Martínez Estrada* (La Plata: Universidad Nacional de la Plata, 1968).

6. Between 1936 and 1945 more than a million people migrated from the Interior provinces of Argentina to the urban center of Buenos Aires; 67 percent of the population thus resides in the capital. See Tulio Halperín Donghi, *Argentina: la democracia de masas* (Buenos Aires: Paidós, 1986); José Luis Romero, *Latinoamérica: las ciudades y las ideas* (Mexico: Siglo XXI, 1976); and Gino Germani,

Estructura social de la Argentina: Análisis estadístico (Buenos Aires: Editorial Raigal, 1955).

7. Aníbal Ford and J. B. Rivera, *Medios de comunicación y cultura popular* (Buenos Aires: Legasa, 1987), 27. See also Jaime Rest, *Literatura y cultura de masas* (Buenos Aires: CEAL, 1967); and Eduardo Romano and Abel Posada, et al., *La cultura popular del peronismo* (Buenos Aires: Editorial Cimarrón, 1974) on the mass media in Argentina during this period.

8. Martínez Estrada's views do not deviate from the conventional distinction between high and low culture, and favor the former.

9. See Néstor García Canclini, "¿Habrá cine latinoamericano en el año 2000? La cultura visual en la época del postnacionalismo." *Domingo* (México) 21 (Febrero 1993): 27–33.

10. Ezequiel Martínez Estrada, *La cabeza de Goliat* (Buenos Aires: CEAL, 1981), 22. Further references to this text are noted parenthetically as CG. Speed as a constitutive element of urban life is a traditional topos and can be found in Karl Marx, Walter Benjamin, and George Simmel. See also Paul Virilio, *Speed and Politics: An Essay on Dromology* (New York: Columbia University Press, 1986) and for Latin America, Nestor García Canclini, *Imaginarios urbanos* (Buenos Aires: EUDEBA, 1997).

11. Samuel Weber, *Mass Mediarus. Form, Technics, Media* (Stanford: Stanford University Press, 1996), 88.

12. For an excellent discussion of the fragment in Benjamin, see Fioretos.

13. Martínez Estrada's notion of degraded vision is quite different from the avant-garde vision described by Francine Masiello, *Las escuelas argentinas de vanguardia* (Buenos Aires: Hachette, 1986), for whom the photographic eye of the poet becomes "una metáfora de la conquista moderna," capable of seeing and controlling the phenomenal world. See especially chapter 4: "Contra la naturaleza: El paisaje de la vanguardia."

14. Both Eduardo Cadava, *Words of Light: Theses on the Photography of History* (Princeton: Princeton University Press, 1997), and Weber point out that in Benjamin's "The Work of Art" essay, mechanical should be translated as technical, according to the original German version.

15. The moment of interruption that Martínez Estrada registers in the city's temporality shows a remarkable likeness to Benjamin's formulation of now-time in "The Work of Art" essay but is devoid of its revolutionary potential.

16. Cadava, *Words of Light*, 25

17. Bhabha, *Nation and Narration*, 299.

18. Alfredo Rubione relates it to "costumbrista" literature and for this reason is the most fictional of Martínez Estrada's essays. See his prologue to *La cabeza de Goliat* (Buenos Aires: CEAL, 1981).

19. González Echevarría, *The Voice of the Masters*, 15–16.

20. The text is full of paradoxes: "Los caminos indicaban las rutas por donde no se debían andar" [The roads indicated the routes on which one should not travel] 55. Martínez Estrada's theories on the paradox as a rhetorical device can be found in a yet unpublished manuscript housed at the Fundación Martínez Estrada (Bahía Blanca). On these materials, see Liliana Weinberg de Magis, *Ezequiel Martínez Estrada y la interpretación del Martín Fierro* (Mexico: UNAM, 1992).

21. The list of visitors to Argentina as of the 1910s is extensive and includes

Ramón del Valle Inclán, Anatole France, Albert Einstein, Waldo Frank, and L. de Corvusier; Count Keyserling is invited by Victoria Ocampo. Ortega y Gasset, who arrived in Argentina in 1916, enjoyed much prestige (he is even said to be responsible for naming the magazine *Sur*), but as of the 1940s his influence begins to wane. In *La cabeza de Goliat*, Martínez Estrada describes the Spanish philosopher in the following manner: "Ortega y Gasset fue, entre nosotros, el primer conferenciante que enseñó el arte magnífico del actor y de la comedia de las ideas" [Ortega y Gasset was, among us, the first lecturer who taught the magnificent art of the actor and the comedy of ideas] 136. In 1950 Patricio Canto shows that Ortega y Gasset's theories are outdated; see his *El caso Ortega y Gasset* (Buenos Aires: Ediciones Leviatán, 1958).

22. The publication of *Sarmiento* was followed in 1947 by *Los invariantes históricos del Facundo* (1947), which were originally two conference papers given in the Librería Viau in honor of the centenary of the publication of *Facundo* in 1875. *Meditaciones sarmientinas* was published posthumously in Mexico in 1968. See Enrique Espinoza, "Notas del compilador," in Ezequiel Martínez Estrada, *Para una revisión de las letras argentinas: prolegómenos* (Buenos Aires: Ed. Losada, 1967).

23. Quoted in John King, *Sur: A Study of the Argentinian Literary Journal and the Development of a Culture* (Cambridge: Cambridge University Press, 1986), 100.

24. See Theodor Adorno and Max Horkheimer, *The Dialectic of Enlightenment* (New York: Continuum, 1987).

25. Ezequiel Martínez Estrada, *Sarmiento* (Buenos Aires: Argos, 1956), 110–11. Further references to this text will be noted parenthetically as S.

26. For the relations between fascism and Enlightenment philosophy, see also Eduardo Subirats, *Figuras de la conciencia desdichada* (Madrid: Taurus, 1979); Hannah Arendt, *The Origins of Totalitarianism* (New York: Harvest/HBJ, 1968); Julia Kristeva, *Strangers to Ourselves* (New York: Columbia University Press, 1991); and Jurgen Habermas, *The Philosophical Discourse of Modernity* (Cambridge: MIT Press, 1990). A more detailed analysis of the concepts of universalism and particularism will be found in chapter 4: "On Being Mexican, for Example: Octavio Paz and the Dialectics of Universality."

27. For the importance of *Martín Fierro* in definitions of national identity, see Carlos Altamirano and Beatriz Sarlo, *Ensayos argentinos: De Sarmiento a la vanguardia* (Buenos Aires: CEAL, 1983); Graciela Montaldo, "Polémicas," in *Historia social de la literatura argentina: Yrigoyen entre Borges y Arlt (1916–1930)* (Buenos Aires: Contrapunto, 1989); and María T. Gramuglio and Beatriz Sarlo, *Martín Fierro y su crítica* (Buenos Aires: CEAL, 1980).

28. Altamirano and Sarlo, *Ensayos argentinos*, 99. On Lugones, also see Jorge Monteleone, Montaldo, "Lugones: Canto Natal del Héroe," in *Historia social de la literatura argentina*; and N. Jitrik, *Leopoldo Lugones: Mito Nacional (*Buenos Aires: Palestra, 1960).

29. G. Perosio and N. Rivarola, "Ricardo Rojas: Primer Profesor de la literatura argentina," in *Historia de la literatura argentina*, vol. 3 (Buenos Aires: CEAL, 1981), 233.

30. Phillipe Lacoue-Labarthe, *Heidegger, Art and Politics* (Oxford: Basil Blackwell, 1990), 64.

31. Leopoldo Lugones, *El payador y anatología de poesía y prosa* (Caracas: Biblioteca Ayacucho, 1979), 200. Further references to this text will be noted parenthetically as P.

32. For the political uses of voice and representation in the gauchesque tradition, see Ludmer.

33. Ezequiel Martínez Estrada, *Muerte y transfiguración de Martín Fierro: Ensayo de interpretación de la vida argentina* (Buenos Aires: CEAL, 1983), 455. Further references to this text are noted parenthetically as MT. *Muerte y transfiguración* is full of ironic allusions to Lugones. If Lugones states in *El payador* (1916), that he never felt so "hijo del país," [son of the nation] Martínez Estrada will state that in the mythifying readings of *Martín Fierro*, the gaucho "es otra vez un redentor, sólo que si antes lo fue de la abyecta condición del gaucho, ahora lo será de la tradición, de las virtudes caballerescas del hijo de la tierra" [is again a redeemer, but if earlier he was the redeemer of the abject condition of the gaucho, he is now one of tradition, of the virtues of the son of the land]. The *payador* is now Lugones.

34. Martínez Estrada's dating of the poem is repeated in Angel Rama's study of gauchesque literature. See *Los gauchipolíticos rioplatenses* (Buenos Aires: CEAL, 1982).

35. Jorge Luis Borges, "Sobre *The Purple Land*," in *Otras Inquisiciones: Obras Completas* (Buenos Aires: Emecé, 1974), 114.

36. Ezequiel Martínez Estrada, *El mundo maravilloso de Guillermo Enrique Hudson* (México: FCE, 1951), 137–38.

37. Both Borges and Martínez Estrada base their comments primarily on Hudson's *The Purple Land* (1885) which thematically develops what these authors consider to be the "strangeness" of Hudson's prose. The wandering through the Uruguayan countryside of the principal character, Richard Lamb, is testimony to the impossibility of literal translations which, in Lamb's case, is followed by the progressive problematization of his sense of identity. See Silvia Rosman, "The Nation in Translation: Of Travelers, Foreigners and Nomads" in *Latin American Literary Review* 26, no. 51 (1998): 17–29.

38. Octavio Paz, *Traducción: literatura y literalidad* (Barcelona Tusquets Editores, 1971), 10.

39. Walter Benjamin, "The Task of the Translator," *Illuminations* (New York: Schocken Books, 1969) 73–74.

40. See Paul De Man, "'Conclusions': Walter Benjamin's 'The Task of the Translator,'" in *The Resistance to Theory* (Minneapolis: University of Minnesota Press, 1986). See also Claude Lévesque, *L'étrangeté du texte* (Montreal: VLB éditeur, 1976) for the unhomely character of translations.

41. Ezequiel Martínez Estrada, *En torno a Kafka y otros ensayos*, ed. E. Espinoza (Barcelona: Seix Barral, 1967). In her study of gauchesque literature Ludmer shows that linguistic violence is constitutive of the genre. The clash between two or more languages is also present in Borges, as we will see in the following chapter. See also Gilles Deleuze and Félix Guattari, *Kafka: Toward a Minor Literature* (Minneapolis: University of Minnesota Press, 1986).

42. Andrej Warminski, *Readings in Interpretation: Hölderlin, Hegel, Heidegger* (Minneapolis: University of Minnesota Press, 1987), lv.

43. Benjamin, "The Task of the Translator," 77.

44. Gilles Deleuze and Félix Guattari, *A Thousand Plateaus: Capitalism and Schizophrenia* (Minneapolis: University of Minnesota Press, 1987), 380. See also G. Deleuze, "Pensée Nomade," *Nietzsche aujoud'hui* (Paris: UGE, 1973).

45. Deleuze and Guattari, *A Thousand Plateaus*, 381.

CHAPTER 3
ON BEING MEXICAN, FOR EXAMPLE: OCTAVIO PAZ
AND THE DIALECTICS OF UNIVERSALITY

1. The notions of particularity and singularity are used interchangeably throughout Paz's essays, although singularity is closer to Paz's notion of "otredad." The displacement of these concepts is discussed throughout the chapter.

2. Octavio Paz, *El laberinto de la soledad,* vol. 8, *Obras Completas* (Mexico: FCE, 1994), 176. Further references to this text are noted parenthetically as LS.

3. Octavio Paz, "En el filo del viento: México y Japón," vol. 8, *Obras Completas*, 414.

4. During the 1940s the "Grupo Hiperión," which promoted the notion of a Mexican philosophy, published a monographic series titled "México y lo mexicano," headed by Leopoldo Zea. See the Claude Fell interview with Paz conducted in 1975, now published as "Vuelta a *El laberinto de la soledad*" in volume 8 of *Obras Completas*, where he refers to this group. For the intellectual history of Paz's texts, see Enrico Mario Santí's excellent study, *El acto de las palabras: Estudios y Diálogos con Octavio Paz* (Mexico: FCE, 1997). See also Ramón Xirau, *Octavio Paz: el sentido de la palabra* (México: J. Mortiz, 1970); Jorge Aguilar Mora, *La divina pareja: Historia y mito. Valoración e interpretación de la obra ensayística de Octavio Paz* (México: Ediciones Era, 1978) and Roberto Hozven, *Octavio Paz: Viajero del Presente* (México: El Colegio Nacional, 1994).

5. This lecture now appears as "Posdata," vol. 8, *Obras Completas*. Further references to this text are noted parenthetically as PD.

6. Quoted in Santí, *El acto*, 145–46. It is important to note that the United Nations was founded in 1945, partly because of the belief in the decline of the Nation-State in the post-war period. For an analysis of Mexican history during the post-war period, see Pablo González Casanova, coord., *América Latina: Historia de Medio Siglo 2. Centroamérica, México y el Caribe* (Mexico: Siglo XXI, 1981) and for the internationalist thrust of postnational thought, see Michael Hardt and Antonio Negri, *Empire* (Cambridge: Harvard University Press, 2000).

7. The notion of example is linked also to the problematic of the moral essay that, in the interview with Fell, Paz says to have been a model for *El laberinto de la soledad*.

8. My comments on the function of examples and exemplarity are based, in whole and in part, on Alexander Gelley, ed., *Unruly Examples: On the Rhetoric of Exemplarity* (Stanford: Stanford University Press, 1995); Ewa Ziarek, "'The Beauty of Failure': Kafka and Benjamin on the Task of Transmission and Translation," in *Unruly Examples*; and Thomas Keenan, *Fables of Responsibilities: Aber-*

rations and Predicaments in Ethics and Politics (Stanford: Stanford University Press, 1997).

9. Gelley, *Unruly Examples*, 2–3.

10. For Gelley, "it is the outward reach to an agency of reception that constitutes the rhetorical [pragmatic?] dimension of the example," *Unruly Examples*, 3.

11. The use of key words such as "necessity," "self-consciousness," and "dialectics" points to the influence of Hegel and Marx in the essay. As we will see, these, as well as many other keywords or concepts, suffer considerable dissemination throughout the essay. See Santí on Paz's sources for *El laberinto de la soledad*.

12. On this issue, see Santí, *El acto*, and Alberto Moreiras, "Alternancia México/Mundo en la posición crítica de Octavio Paz," in *Nueva Revista de Filología Hispánica* (México) 35, no. 1 (1987): 251–64.

13. Yet another way to think the duality of the example is to say that it is both dialectical and undecidable. See note 37 for a definition of undecidability.

14. As is well known, Paz earned considerable criticism for what many perceived to be his racist and classist characterization of the *pachuco*.

15. Santí emphasizes the psychoanalytical reading of the *pachuco* as a structuring principle throughout the essay: the *pachuco*'s neurosis is prototypical of the rest of the nation. While this reading is an important one, our study aims to see how in the essay the very notion of what is prototypical (i.e. exemplary) is precisely the problem being put into question.

16. Brett Levinson, *Secondary Moderns: Mimesis, History and Revolution in Lezama Lima's "American Expression"* (Lewisburg, Pa.: Bucknell University Press, 1996), also studies the notion of model or law in Paz.

17. For the rhetoric of failure in relation to the notion of example, see Ziarek.

18. Paz rejects the Hegelian dialectic outright in *El arco y la lira*. See the Claude Fell interview already cited.

19. Paz, "Vuelta a *El laberinto de la soledad*," vol. 8, *Obras Completas*, 245.

20. Nancy, *Inoperative Community*, 45. See also Claude Lévi-Strauss, Georges Bataille, Roger Callois, Marcel Mauss, and Emile Durkheim.

21. Santí makes a similar point regarding myths, but emphasizes myths' role in the "collective psyche" and their still sacred function: "esos mitos antiguos no son, propiamente, el objeto del ensayo. La máscara, la Fiesta, el culto a la muerte, el grito obsceno, que son los estudiados, no forman . . . tanto instancias de una mitología cuanto manifestaciones cotidianas de la vida moderna, síntomas hasta cierto punto insólitos de una psique colectiva que muestra la supervivencia de lo sagrado" [those ancient myths are not exactly the object of the essay. The mask, the Celebration, the cult of death, the obscene cry that are studied do not compose . . . the instances of a mythology, but rather daily manifestations of modern life, unusual symptoms, up to a certain point, of a collective psyche that shows the survival of the sacred], *El acto*, 195.

22. On modernity and myth, see Adorno and Horkheimer, *The Dialectic of Enlightenment* and Jean-François Lyotard, *The Postmodern Condition*.

23. Although I principally discuss Laclau's formulations due to the similarities they share with Paz's argument, many critics have discussed the concepts of universality and particularity in relation to the question of identity. See especially E. Balibar and I. Wallerstein, *Race Nation, Class: Ambiguous Identities* (London:

Verso, 1991); J. Rancière, *On the Shores of Politics* (London: Verso, 1995); and Derrida, *The Other Heading*.

24. In *Emancipation(s)* Laclau bases his use of constitutive lack on Lacan's formulation of the symbolic identification that designates the production of the subject of the unconscious. The singularity of a signifying life is given by a mark which is exterior to us but of which we are dispossessed (it is lacking). For excellent discussions of identification in Freud and Lacan, see David Nasio, *Enseñanza de Siete Conceptos Centrales* (Barcelona: Gedisa, 1996), as well as Diana Fuss, *Identification Papers* (London: Routledge, 1995).

25. For a discussion of Laclau and Mouffe, see Anna Marie Smith, *Laclau and Mouffe: The Radical Democratic Imaginary* (London: Routledge, 1998).

26. Laclau, *Emancipation(s)*, 34–35.

27. For Laclau democracy can be thought only as the agonistic relation of competing groups that at certain moments give their particularism universal representation. This formulation, which posits that the universal exists as a horizon and not as a body (a representation itself), appears problematic given that one could think of the demands of repressive and even totalitarian groups as a particularism given universal representation. In response to a critique by Claude Lefort, Laclau admits the possibility of this occurring. Nevertheless, a key element for Laclau is that the universal's temporary and changing status avoids the solidification of the universal, which has been the reason behind almost every type of repression which modernity has known.

28. The question that Paz formulates speaks to what in a 1993 note to this chapter of the essay Paz calls his hope for a socialist alternative in Latin America. As of the 1940s, Paz's dissatisfaction with socialism is well known. See José Quiroga, *Understanding Octavio Paz* (Columbia: University of South Carolina Press, 1999).

29. In this sense radical democratic politics as formulated by Laclau (and Chantal Mouffe) would differentiate itself from both liberal and communitarian theories of the social. See Linda M. G. Zerilli, "The Universalism Which is Not One," *Diacritics* 28, no. 2 (1998): 3–20.

30. Santí notes that the importance Paz places on the function of poetry in relation to Mexican history and traditions appears in essays later published as *Primeras letras (1931–1943)*, as well as in later texts. See "Introducción a *Primeras Letras*."

31. For Heidegger "Poetry is the founding naming of Being and of the essence of all things . . . Poetry is the originary language of a historical people," quoted in Leslie Hill, *Blanchot: Extreme Contemporary* (London: Routledge, 1997). Heidegger's texts (especially *Being and Time*) are an important influence on Paz throughout *El arco y la lira*, although by the second edition his disagreements with the German philosopher will become more pronounced. Paz was exposed to Heidegger's thought through José Gaos's translations into Spanish.

32. Octavio Paz, *El arco y la lira*, vol. 1, *Obras Completas* (Mexico: FCE, 1994). Further references to this text are noted parenthetically as AL. All translations of this text correspond to Octavio Paz, *The Bow and the Lyre*, trans. Ruth Simms (Austin: University of Texas press, 1973), 235. Some translations have been modified and those with no page numbers are my own.

33. *El arco y la lira* is based in part on a 1942 lecture titled "Poesía de la soledad y poesía de la comunión." In the prologue to his *Obras Completas, La casa de la presencia*, which includes *El arco y la lira*, Paz speaks of this early

essay and calls its discussion of modernity and poetry "simplista y sumaria" [simplistic and summary], 22.

34. See Santí, "Crítica y política: 'El arco y la lira' y el poeta crítico." In a 1989 interview in Japan, Paz insists on the priority of the voice over writing, see vol. 8, *Obras Completas*, 414.

35. The notion of undecidability is developed by Jacques Derrida following Kurt Gödel's theorem regarding undecidable propositions. Rodolphe Gasché explains the term: "*undecidable* must be understood to refer not only to essential incompleteness and inconsistency, bearing in mind their distinction from ambiguity, but also to indicate a level vaster than that which is encompassed by the opposition between what is decidable and undecidable . . . Their undecidability [i.e. of opposites], their "floating indetermination" permits the substitution and the play of the conceptual binary oppositions, which, by turning into one another, become incapable of denominating and defining the medium from which they emerge." See his *The Tain of the Mirror: Derrida and the Philosophy of Reflection* (Cambridge: Harvard University Press, 1986), 241–42.

36. The writer Juan José Saer echoes Paz's thoughts in "Exilio y literatura," in *El concepto de ficción* (Buenos Aires: Ariel, 1997).

37. See Paul De Man, "Heidegger's exegesis of Holderlin" in *Blindness and Insight*. For an analysis of the notion of passivity, especially in the work of E. Levinas, M. Blanchot and G. Agamben, see Thomas C. Wall, *Radical Passivity* (Albany: SUNY Press, 1999).

38. This recalls the Nietzchean appeal to getting one's ears ready to be able to hear the unheard-of.

39. Weber, *Mass Mediauras*, 78–79.

40. Martin Heidegger, "The Age of the World Picture," in *The Question Concerning Technology and other Essays*, trans. W. Lovitt (New York: Harper and Row, 1977).

41. Ibid, 134, 136.

42. My discussion of the image is based on Marie-Claire Ropars-Wuilleumier, *L'idée d'image* (Vincennes: PUV, 1995).

43. Maurice Blanchot, *The Infinite Conversation*, trans. Susan Hanson (Minneapolis: University of Minnesota Press, 1992).

44. Paz's notion of the poetic image sheds light on his discussion of the *pachuco* in *El laberinto de la soledad*. Just like Narcissus, Paz's *pachuco* defies the law of identity.

45. I discuss Benjamin's notion of *jetzseit* at length in the introduction.

46. For a detailed discussion of the relations between poetry, revolution and rebellion, a discussion of which lies outside the scope of this chapter, see Paz's *Los hijos del limo*.

47. In *Dis-agreement*, Rancière develops the notion of disagreement in order to draw the outlines of the political as a singular event not sutured to other fields of knowledge or discursive practices.

CHAPTER 4

BORGES: ON READING, TRANSLATION, AND
THE IMPOSSIBILITY OF NAMING

1. Parts of this chapter were first presented as a conference paper titled "Traducción y nación en Borges: Una relación imposible," in celebration of Borges's centenary at New York University, April 1999.

2. Jorge Luis Borges, *El idioma de los argentinos* (Buenos Aires: Seix Barral, 1994), 136. Further references to this text are noted parenthetically as IA. Translations are my own.

3. For a suggestive reference to orality and translation in Borges, see Jaime Concha, "El Aleph: Borges y la historia" in *Revista Iberoamericana* (Apr–Sept 1983) 49: 471–85.

4. Jorge Luis Borges, "Los traductores de las 1001 noches," in *Historia de la Eternidad*, vol. 1, *Obras Completas* (Buenos Aires: Emecé Editores, 1974), 400. Translations of Borges's non-fictions are from Jorge Luis Borges, *Selected Non-Fictions*, ed. E. Weinberger (New York: Viking, 1999). Page references to this text are noted parenthetically; otherwise translations are my own.

5. Jorge Luis Borges, "Las versiones homéricas," in *Discusión*, vol. 1, *Obras Completas*, 239. Further references to this text are noted parenthetically as VH. The question of translation is directly and indirectly thematized in "Las versiones homéricas," "El acercamiento a Altomásim," "Tlon, Uqbar, Orbis Tertius," "Emma Zunz," "Deutsches Requiem," "La busca de Averroes," and many other texts.

6. In his study of Walter Benjamin's essay "The Task of the Translator" in *The Resistance to Theory*, Paul DeMan describes the difference between nomination and intention in terms of the difference between logos and lexis.

7. Jorge Luis Borges, "El libro," in *Borges Oral*, vol. 4, *Obras Completas* (Buenos Aires: Emecé Editores, 1996), 169.

8. See Jacques Derrida, "Plato's Pharmacy," in *Dissemination* (Chicago: University of Chicago Press, 1981).

9. See Jacques Derrida, *The Ear of the Other: Otobiography, Transference, Translation*, ed. Christie McDonald (Lincoln: University of Nebraska Press, 1985).

10. Perhaps with Borges's "El aleph" in mind, the editors of the Biblioteca Ayacucho edition of *El payador*, which also includes selections of Lugones's poetry, note that the excerpt from *Odas Seculares* cannot be included in its totality because of its extensive length.

11. For an analysis of the relations between nationalism and Lugones's poetry, see María Teresa Gramuglio, "Literatura y nacionalismo: Leopoldo Lugones y la construcción de imágenes de escritor," in *Hispamérica*. Año XXII. Abril/agosto 1993. No. 64/65: 5–17, as well as Enrique Zuleta Alvarez, "Borges, Lugones y el nacionalismo," in *Cuadernos Hispanoamericanos: Revista Mensual de Cultura Hispánica* (Madrid) July–Sept. 1992): 505–7, 535–49. See also Borges's own studies of Lugones, *Leopoldo Lugones* (Buenos Aires: Troquel, 1955) and the prologue to *El Hacedor* (Buenos Aires: Emecé, 1960).

12. Maria Luisa Bastos, *Borges Ante la Crítica Argentina, 1923–1960* (Buenos Aires: Ediciones Hispamérica, 1974), 146. See also Jorge Panesi, "Borges y la cultura italiana en la argentina," in *Críticas* (Buenos Aires: Norma, 2000).

13. An exact dating of "El escritor argentino y la tradición" is unavailable, but it was most likely written one or two years after "El aleph." The essay was first published in *Sur* in 1955.

14. Ricardo Piglia, "Existe la novela argentina?" in *Crítica y ficción* (Buenos Aires: Siglo Veinte, 1990), 50.

15. Ibid., 51.

16. In her *Borges, un escritor en las orillas* (Buenos Aires: Ariel, 1995), Beatriz Sarlo reads Borges in a similar way.

17. For an analysis of "El escritor argentino y la tradición" on which my own reading relies, see Sandra Contreras, "Variaciones sobre el escritor argentino y la tradición," in *Borges ocho ensayos*, ed. S. Cueto, A. Giordano, and others (Rosario: Beatriz Viterbo Editora, 1995).

18. In his introduction to *The Spanish American Regional Novel*, Carlos Alonso notes that for Borges nationalist longings for autochthonous texts are always doomed to failure given the self-reflexive distance that must necessarily intervene in the cultural production of that autochthonous text. The "nature of the project of cultural definition" thus ironically becomes complicit with its non-realization. I am in agreement with Alonso but differ in emphasis. What he calls the distance implied in the self-reflexive gesture of all cultural projects (anthropological ones being the example he privileges) I read at the level of language in Borges's texts. For Borges it is language, even one's own language, which institutes that distance and not necessarily an agent (the writer) or the effects of cultural definitions.

19. Jorge Luis Borges, "El escritor argentino y la tradición," in *Discusión*, vol. 1, *Obras Completas*, 270–71. Further references to this this text are noted parenthetically as EA.

20. Similarly, in *The Ear of the Other* Derrida shows how Borges's "Pierre Menard, Autor del Quijote" is "very subtly marked by a certain Frenchness," 99.

21. In his reading of Edgar Allan Poe's "The Purloined Letter," Jacques Lacan describes the symbolic structure as a chain effect produced by the constant displacement of the signifier (the letter). In Poe's story the signified of the signifier remains elusive. For Borges, as for Lacan, the indeterminacy of the signifier is constitutive of writing. See Lacan's "Le séminaire sur 'La Lettre volée,'" in *Ecrits* (Paris: Seuil, 1966), 11–61 and Jacques Derrida's analysis of Lacan's text in *The Post Card* (Chicago: University of Chicago Press, 1987), 413–96.

22. Jorge Luis Borges, "El aleph," in *El Aleph*, vol. 1, *Obras Completas*, 624. Further references to this text are noted parenthetically as A. Translations of Borges's fictional texts throughout this chapter are from Jorge Luis Borges, *Collected Fictions*, trans. A. Hurley (New York: Viking, 1998). Page references to this text appear parenthetically; otherwise the translations are mine.

23. My remarks on the Tower of Babel are based on Derrida's *The Ear of the Other*.

24. This definition of myth can be read from J. G. Frazer and C. Lévi-Strauss to S. Freud and C. Jung. For an interesting discussion of myth, see Marcel Hénaff, *Claude Lévi-Strauss and the Making of Structural Anthropology* (Minneapolis: University of Minnesota Press, 1998).

25. See Nancy, "Myth Interrupted," in *The Inoperative Community*.

26. In *A View from Afar* (Chicago: University of Chicago Press, 1993), Lévi-Strauss states: "A myth proposes a grid, definable only by its rules of construction. For the participants in the culture to which the myth belongs, this grid confers a meaning not on the myth itself but on everything else: that is, on the images of the world, of society, and of its history, of which the members of the group are more or less aware," 145–46.

27. For the notion of Nazi myth and its importance for fascist aestheticism, see Lacoue-Labarthe. See also Walter Benjamin, "The Work of Art in the Age of Mechanical Reproduction."

28. Quoted in Nidia Burgos, "Los intelectuales argentinos del grupo Sur ante la

Segunda Guerra Mundial" in *La Argentina y Europa (1930–1950) II* (Bahía Blanca: Departamento de Humanidades, Universidad Nacional del Sur, 1998), 76. Interestingly, abjection ("ruinas", "envilecimiento") points both to the defeat and victory of the Germans. This apparently innocuous statement by Borges is in line with Julia Kristeva's analysis of abjection in *Powers of Horror* (New York: Columbia University Press, 1982). According to Kristeva, Borges writes the infamy of fascism as the infamy of writing: abjection destroys the subject/object relation of traditional representation and the Aleph is thus the "figure" of writing as abjection. An analysis of infamy in Borges is beyond the scope of this study. Borges published numerous articles against fascism in *Sur* from 1937–45, as well as in *La Nación* and *El hogar*. "Deutsches Requiem" in *El Aleph* is a short story whose theme is Nazi fascism.

29. Benjamin, "The Task of the Translator," 73–74.

30. Juan B. Ritvo makes this point in his *La edad de la lectura* (Rosario: Beatriz Viterbo Editora, 1992).

31. Hill, *Blanchot: Extreme Contemporary*, 113.

32. Maurice Blanchot, *The Space of Literature* (Lincoln: University of Nebraska Press, 1989), 32.

33. Sylvia Molloy, *Las letras de Borges y otros ensayos* (Rosario: Beatriz Viterbo Editora, 1999), 67–68. Molloy's excellent book is still one of the few authoritative studies on Borges. See also Kadir's *Questing Fictions*, especially chapter 10, "Borges's Ghost Writer."

34. Jorge Luis Borges, "La muralla y los libros," in *Otras inquisiciones*, vol. 2, *Obras Completas* (Buenos Aires: Emecé Editores, 1974), 13.

35. Jorge Luis Borges, "El muerto," in *El Aleph*, vol. 1, *Obras Completas*, 549.

36. See Molloy's astute critique of Foucault in *Las letras de Borges*, chapter 7: "El soterrado cimiento."

37. See Guillermo Martínez, "Rescate de unas cartas obscenas," *Clarín: Cultura y Nación* (Buenos Aires), 22 August 1999.

38. My comments on prosopopeia are based on Paul DeMan's "Hypogram and Inscription," in *The Resistance to Theory*.

39. DeMan, "Hypogram and Inscription," 48.

40. In the Kabbalah, the aleph is the first letter of the book of Creation, the Sefer Yezirah, and thus points to the truth of the divine ("emet"). However, the erasure of the first letter of this word (the aleph) signifies death. Birth and death cohabit the aleph. See Gershom Scholem, *Kabbalah*. New York: Penguin, 1978. See also Borges's "El golem" in *El otro, el mismo*; "Una vindicación de la cábala" in *Discusión*; and "La cábala" in *Siete noches*.

41. Alberto Moreiras understands the effects of the closure of metaphysics as constituting an integral part of a certain Latin American cultural production, among which he includes Borges's texts: "los textos estudiados incidirían en un tercer espacio donde las relaciones entre figuralidad literaria y perspectiva teórica están radicalmente problematizadas a partir de la experiencia del fin de la promesa ontoteológica; consecuentemente, todos ellos, también, se constituyen como textos a partir de una experiencia básica o extrema de pérdida del fundamento que de una forma u otra tematizan; por último, todos ellos hacen del lugar de la pérdida el lugar de una cierta recuperación, siempre precaria e inestable, pues siempre constituída sobre un abismo" [the texts studied would fall in a third space where the

relations between literary figuration and theoretical perspective are radically prob-lematized due to the experience of the end of the onto-theological promise; conse-quently, all of them make of the place of that loss the place of a certain recuperation, always precarious and unstable, because it is constructed over the abyss], in *Tercer Espacio: Literatura y Duelo en América Latina* (Santiago: Universidad Arcis, 1999), 25.

42. See the classic study on this topic, Marcel Mauss's *The Gift: The Form and Reason for Exchange in Archaic Societies* (New York: Norton, 1990).

CONCLUDING REMARKS

1. Allusions to "El aleph" are many: Beatriz reappears as the narrator's lover, the library of the future congress is stored in a basement and later destroyed, the notion of a "shared" language is repeated.

2. I am here referring to Giorgio Agamben, *The Coming Community* (Minneapolis: Minnesota University Press, 1993).

3. Jorge Luis Borges, "El congreso," *El libro de arena*, vol. 3, *Obras Completas* (Buenos Aires: Emecé, 1989), 23. Further references are noted parenthetically as C. Translations are based on Jorge Luis Borges, *Collected Fictions*, trans. A. Hurley and are noted parenthetically.

4. For the notion of ruins in Benjamin, see his *The Origin of German Tragic Drama* and "Central Park."

5. See J. Hillis Miller, *Reading Narrative* (Norman: University of Oklahoma Press, 1998).

6. See Slavoj Žižek, *The Ticklish Subject* (London: Verso, 1999).

Works Cited

ALEJO CARPENTIER

Obras Completas. Vol. 2. Mexico: Siglo XXI, 1997.
Obras Completas. Vols. 10 and 11. Mexico: Siglo XXI, 1987.
Razón de ser: Ensayos. Mexico: Siglo XXI, 1990.

Criticism:

Colás, Santiago. "'Dangerous Southern Islands': Modern Aesthetics as Anaesthetics in Carpentier's *The Lost Steps* and Borges's 'The South.'" In *Modernism and its Margins: Reinscribing Cultural Modernity from Spain and Latin America,* edited by A. Geist and J. Monleón. New York: Garland, 1999.

González, Eduardo. *Alejo Carpentier: el tiempo del hombre.* Caracas: Monte Avila, 1978.

González Echevarría, Roberto. *Alejo Carpentier: The Pigrim at Home.* Ithaca: Cornell University Press, 1990.

Kadir, Djelal. *Questing Fictions: Latin America's Family Romance.* Minneapolis: University of Minnesota Press, 1986.

López-Baralt, Mercedes. "Los pasos encontrados de Levi-Strauss y Alejo Carpentier: literatura y antropología en el siglo veinte." *Revista del Centro de Estudios Avanzados de Puerto Rico y el Caribe* 7 (Jul–Dec. 1988).

Millington, Mark. "Gender Monologue in Carpentier's *Los pasos perdidos.*" *MLN* 111 (1996).

Pérez Firmat, Gustavo. "El lenguaje secreto de *Los pasos perdidos.*" *MLN* 99 (1984).

Taylor, Karen. "La creación musical en *Los pasos perdidos.*" *Nueva Revista de Filología Hispánica* 26 (1977).

EZEQUIEL MARTÍNEZ ESTRADA

La cabeza de Goliat. Buenos Aires: CEAL, 1981.
Muerte y transfiguración de Martín Fierro: Ensayo de interpretación de la vida argentina. Buenos Aires: CEAL, 1983.
El mundo maravilloso de Guillermo Enrique Hudson. México: FCE, 1951.
Radiografía de la pampa. Buenos Aires: Losada, 1976.

Sarmiento. Buenos Aires: Argos, 1946.

En torno a Kafka y otros ensayos, edited by E. Espinoza. Barcelona: Seix Barral, 1967.

Criticism:

Adam, Carlos. *Bibliografía y documentos de Ezequiel Martínez Estrada.* La Plata: Universidad Nacional de la Plata, 1968.

Altamirano, Carlos, and Beatriz Sarlo. *Ensayos argentinos: De Sarmiento a la vanguardia.* Buenos Aires: CEAL, 1983.

Espinoza, Enrique, ed. "Notas del compilador" to *Para una revisión de las letras argentinas: prolegómenos,* by Ezequiel Martínez Estrada. Buenos Aires: Ed. Losada, 1967.

Montaldo, Graciela. *De pronto, el campo: Literatura argentina y tradición rural.* Rosario: Beatriz Viterbo Editora, 1993.

Rama, Angel. *Los gauchipolíticos rioplatenses.* Buenos Aires: CEAL, 1982.

Rosman, Silvia. "The Nation in Translation: Of Travelers, Foreigners and Nomads." *Latin American Literary Review* 26, no. 51 (1998).

Rubione, Alfredo. Prologue to *La cabeza de Goliat* by Ezequiel Martínez Estrada. Buenos Aires: CEAL, 1981.

Viñas, David. *Literatura argentina y política. De Lugones a Walsh.* Buenos Aires: Ed. Sudamericana, 1996.

Weinberg de Magis, Liliana. *Ezequiel Martínez Estrada y la interpretación del Martín Fierro.* Mexico: UNAM, 1992.

OCTAVIO PAZ

Obras Completas. Vols. 1 and 8. Mexico: FCE, 1994.

The Bow and the Lyre. Translated by Ruth Simms. Austin: University of Texas Press, 1973.

Traducción: literatura y literalidad. Barcelona: Tusquets Editores, 1971.

Criticism:

Aguilar Mora, Jorge. *La divina pareja: Historia y mito. Valoración e interpretación de la obra ensayística de Octavio Paz.* México: Ediciones Era, 1978.

Hozven, Roberto. *Octavio Paz: Viajero del Presente.* México: El Colegio Nacional, 1994.

Levinson, Brett. *Secondary Moderns: Mimesis, History and Revolution in Lezama Lima's "American Expression."* Lewisburg, Pa.: Bucknell University Press, 1996.

Moreiras, Alberto. "Alternancia México/Mundo en la posición crítica de Octavio Paz." *Nueva Revista de Filología Hispánica* (México), 1987.

Quiroga, José. *Understanding Octavio Paz*. Columbia: University of South Carolina Press, 1999.

Santí, Enrico Mario. *El acto de las palabras: Estudios y Diálogos con Octavio Paz*. Mexico: FCE, 1997.

Vital, A. "Borges, Paz y Rulfo: Postmodernidad, Modernidad y Contra-Modernidad." *Alba de América* 12 (July 1994): 22–23.

Xirau, Ramón. *Octavio Paz: el sentido de la palabra*. México: J. Mortiz, 1970.

JORGE LUIS BORGES

Collected Fiction. Translated by A. Hurley. New York: Viking, 1998.

El idioma de los argentinos. Buenos Aires: Seix Barral, 1994.

Leopoldo Lugones. Buenos Aires: Troquel, 1955.

Obras Completas. Vols. 1, 2, and 3. Buenos Aires: Emecé Editores, 1974.

Obras Completas. Vol. 4. Buenos Aires: Emecé Editores, 1996.

Prologue, *El Hacedor*. Buenos Aires: Emecé, 1960.

Selected Non-Fictions. Edited by E. Weinberger. New York: Viking, 1999.

El tamaño de mi esperanza. Buenos Aires: Seix Barral, 1993.

Criticism:

Bastos, Maria Luisa. *Borges Ante la Crítica Argentina, 1923–1960*. Buenos Aires: Ediciones Hispamérica, 1974.

Concha, Jaime. "El Aleph: Borges y la historia." *Revista Iberoamericana* 49 (Apr–Sept 1983).

Contreras, Sandra. "Variaciones sobre el escritor argentino y la tradición." In *Borges ocho ensayos*, edited by S. Cueto, A. Giordano, and others. Rosario: Beatriz Viterbo Editora, 1995.

Martínez, Guillermo. "Rescate de unas cartas obscenas." *Clarín: Cultura y Nación*. (Buenos Aires), 22 August 1999.

Molloy, Sylvia. *Las letras de Borges y otros ensayos*. Rosario: Beatriz Viterbo Editora, 1999.

Moreiras, Alberto. *Tercer Espacio: Literatura y Duelo en América Latina*. Santiago: Universidad Arcis, 1999.

Panesi, Jorge. "Borges y la cultura italiana en la argentina." In *Críticas*. Buenos Aires: Norma, 2000.

Piglia, Ricardo. "Existe la novela argentina?" In *Crítica y ficción*. Buenos Aires: Siglo Veinte, 1990.

Sarlo, Beatriz. *Borges, un escritor en las orillas*. Buenos Aires: Ariel, 1995.

Zuleta Alvarez, Enrique. "Borges, Lugones y el nacionalismo." *Cuadernos Hispanoameicanos: Revista Mensual de Cultura Hispánica* (Madrid) (July–Sept. 1992): 505–7, 535–49.

OTHER WORKS

Adorno, Theodor, and Max Horkheimer. *The Dialectic of the Enlightenment*. New York: Continuum, 1988.

Agamben, Giorgio. *The Coming Community*. Minneapolis: Minnesota, 1993.

Alonso, Carlos. *The Spanish American Regional Novel, Modernity and Autochthony*. Cambridge: Cambridge University Press, 1990.

————. *The Burden of Modernity: The Rhetoric of Cultural Discourse in Spanish America*. Oxford: Oxford University Press, 1998.

Anderson, Benedict. *Imagined Communities: Reflections on the Origin and Spread of Nationalism*. London: Verso, 1983.

Apter, Emily. *Continental Drift: From National Characters to Virtual Subjects*. Chicago: University of Chicago Press, 1999

Arendt, Hannah. *The Origins of Totalitarianism*. New York: Harvest/HBJ, 1968.

Bhabha, Homi, ed. *Nation and Narration*. London: Routledge, 1990.

Badiou, Alain. *Manifesto for Philosophy*. Albany: SUNY, 1999.

Balibar, E., and E. Wallerstein. *Race, Nation, Class: Ambiguous Identities*. London: Verso, 1991.

Bello, Andrés. "Gramática castellana." In *Obras Completas*. Caracas, 1951.

Benjamin, Walter. *Illuminations*. New York: Schocken Books, 1969.

Blanchot, Maurice. *The Infinite Conversation*. Translated by Susan Hanson. Minneapolis: University of Minnesota Press, 1992.

————. *Le pas au-dela*. Paris: Gallimard, 1973.

————. *The Space of Literature*. Translated by Ann Smock. Lincoln: University of Nebraska Press, 1989

————. *The Unavowable Community*. Translated by Pierre Joris. New York: Station Hill Press, 1988.

Cadava, Eduardo. *Words of Light: Theses on the Photography of History*. Princeton: Princeton University Press, 1997.

Canto, Patricio. *El caso Ortega y Gasset*. Buenos Aires: Ediciones Leviatán, 1958.

Castoriadis, Cornelius. *The Imaginary Institution of Society*. Cambridge: Polity Press, 1972.

Chiampi, Irlemar. *Barroco y modernidad*. Mexico: FCE, 2000.

De la Campa, Román. *Latin Americanism*. Minneapolis: University of Minnesota Press, 1999.

Deleuze, Gilles. "Pensée Nomade." In *Nietzsche aujoud'hui*. Paris: UGE, 1973.

Deleuze, Gilles, and Félix Guattari. *Kafka: Toward a Minor Literature*. Minneapolis: University of Minnesota Press, 1986.

————. *A Thousand Plateaus: Capitalism and Schizophrenia*. Minneapolis: University of Minnesota Press, 1987.

De Man, Paul. *The Resistance to Theory*. Minneapolis: University of Minnesota Press, 1986.

————. *Blindness and Insight: Essays in the Rhetoric of Contemporary Criticism*. Minneapolis: University of Minnesota Press, 1983.

Derrida, Jacques. *Dissemination*. Translated by B. Johnson. Chicago: University of Chicago Press, 1981.

———. *The Post Card*. Translated by Alan Bass. Chicago: University of Chicago Press, 1987.

———. *The Other Heading: Reflections on Today's Europe*. Translated by P. Brault and M. Nass. Bloomington: Indiana University Press, 1992.

Fioretos, Aris. "Contraction (Benjamin, Reading, History)." *MLN* 110 (1995).

Ford, Aníbal, and J. B. Rivera. *Medios de comunicación y cultura popular*. Buenos Aires: Legasa, 1987.

Franco, Jean. "The Nation as Imagined Community." In *The New Historicism*, edited by H. Aram Veeser. New York: Routledge, 1989.

García Canclini, Nestor. "¿ Habrá cine latinoamericano en el año 2000? La cultura visual en la época del postnacionalismo." *Domingo* (México) 21, Febrero 1993.

———. *Imaginarios Urbanos*. Buenos Aires: EUDEBA, 1997.

Gasché, Rodolphe. *The Tain of the Mirror: Derrida and the Philosophy of Reflection*. Cambridge: Harvard University Press, 1986.

Gelley, Alexander, ed. *Unruly Examples: On the Rhetoric of Exemplarity*. Stanford: Stanford University Press, 1995.

Germani, Gino. *Estructura social de la Argentina: Análisis estadístico*. Buenos Aires: Editorial Raigal, 1955.

González Casanova, Pablo, coord. *América Latina: Historia de Medio Siglo. 2. Centroamérica, México y el Caribe*. Mexico: Siglo XXI, 1981.

González Echevarría, Roberto. *The Voice of the Masters: Writing and Authority in Modern Latin American Literature*. Austin: University of Texas Press, 1985.

Gramuglio, María T. "Literatura y nacionalismo: Leopoldo Lugones y la construcción de imágenes de escritor." *Hispamérica* 64/65 (Abril/agosto 1993).

Gramuglio, María T., and B. Sarlo. *Martín Fierro y su crítica*. Buenos Aires: CEAL, 1980.

Habermas, Jürgen. *The Philosophical Discourse of Modernity*. Cambridge: MIT Press, 1990.

Halperín Donghi, Tulio. *Argentina: la democracia de masas*. Buenos Aires: Paidós, 1986.

Hardt, Michael, and Antonio Negri. *Empire*. Cambridge: Harvard University Press, 2000.

Heidegger, Martin. "The Age of the World Picture." In *The Question Concerning Technology and other Essays*, translated by W. Lovitt. New York: Harper and Row, 1977.

Hénaff, Marcel. *Claude Lévi-Strauss and the Making of Structural Anthropology*. Minneapolis: University of Minnesota Press, 1998.

Henríquez Ureña, Pedro. *Las corrientes literarias en la América Hispana*. Mexico: FCE, 1954.

Hill, Leslie. *Blanchot: Extreme Contemporary*. London: Routledge, 1997.

Irigaray, Luce. *Speculum of the Other Woman*. Ithaca: Cornell University Press, 1985.

Jay, Martin. *Downcast Eyes*. Berkeley: University of California Press, 1994.

Jitrik, Noé. *Leopoldo Lugones: Mito Nacional*. Buenos Aires: Palestra, 1960.

Keenan, Thomas. *Fables of Responsibilities: Aberrations and Predicaments in Ethics and Politics*. Stanford: Stanford University Press, 1997.

King, John. *Sur: A Study of the Argentinian Literary Journal and the Development of a Culture*. Cambridge: Cambridge University Press, 1986

Kristeva, Julia. *Strangers to Ourselves*. New York: Columbia University Press, 1991.

———. *Nations Without Nationalism*. New York: Columbia University Press, 1993.

Lacan Jacques. *Ecrits*. Paris: Seuil, 1966.

Laclau, Ernesto. *Emancipation(s)*. London: Verso, 1996.

Lacoue-Labarthe, Phillipe. *Heidegger, Art and Politics*. Oxford: Basil Blackwell, 1990.

Lévesque, Claude. *L'étrangeté du texte*. Montreal: VLB éditeur, 1976.

Lévi-Strauss, Claude. *A View from Afar*. Translated by J. Neugroschel and P. Hoss. Chicago: University of Chicago Press, 1993.

Lugones, Leopoldo. *El payador*. Caracas: Biblioteca Ayacucho, 1979.

Ludmer, Josefina. *El género gauchesco. Un tratado sobre la patria*. Buenos Aires: Sudamericana, 1988.

Lyotard, Jean-Francois. *The Postmodern Condition: A Report on Knowledge*. Minneapolis: University of Minnesota Press, 1984.

MacCannell, Dean. *The Tourist: A New Theory of the Leisure Class*. New York: Schocken Books, 1976.

Masiello, Francine. *Las escuelas argentinas de vanguardia*. Buenos Aires: Hachette, 1986.

Mauss, Marcel. *The Gift: The Form and Reason for Exchange in Archaic Societies*. New York: Norton, 1990.

Mead, Robert. *Breve historia del ensayo en la América Hispana*. Mexico: DeAndrea, 1956.

Meyer, Doris, ed. *Reinterpreting the Spanish American Essay. Women's Writing of the 19th* and 20th Centuries. Austin: University of Texas Press, 1995.

Miller, J. Hillis. "Literary Study in the Transnational University." In *Black Holes: J. Hillis Miller; or, Boustrophedonic Reading*, edited by Manuel Asensi. Stanford: Stanford University Press, 1999.

———. *Reading Narrative*. Norman: University of Oklahoma Press, 1998.

Molloy, Sylvia. *At Face Value: Autobiographical Writing in Spanish America*. New York: Cambridge University Press, 1991.

Monteleone, Jorge. "Lugones: Canto Natal del Héroe." In *Historia social de la literatura argentina: Yrigoyen, entre Borges y Arlt (1916–1930)*, edited by G. Montaldo. Buenos Aires: Contrapunto, 1989.

Moreiras, Alberto. "Pastiche Identity, and Allegory of Allegory." In *Latin American Identity and Constructions of Difference*, edited by Amaryll Chanady. Minneapolis: University of Minnesota Press, 1993.

Nancy, Jean Luc. *The Inoperative Community*. Minneapolis: University of Minnesota Press, 1991.

Nass, Michael. "Stumping the Sun: Toward a Postmetaphorics." In *Cultural Semiosis: Tracing the Signifier*, edited by Hugh Silverman. New York: Routledge, 1998.

Pease, Donald, ed. *National Identities and Post-Nationalist Narratives*. Durham, N.C.: Duke University Press, 1994.

———. "National Narratives, Postnational Narration" *Modern Fiction Studies* 43, no. 1 (1997): 1–23.

Perosio, Graciela, and N. Rivarola, "Ricardo Rojas. Primer Profesor de la literatura argentina." In *Historia de la literatura argentina*. Vol. 3. Buenos Aires: CEAL, 1981.

Pratt, Mary Louise. *Imperial Eyes. Travel Writing and Transculturation*. London: Routledge, 1992.

Prieto, Adolfo. *Los viajeros ingleses y la emergencia de la literatura argentina*. Buenos Aires: Editorial Sudamericana, 1996.

Rama, Angel. *Transculturación narrativa en América Latina*. Mexico: Siglo XXI, 1982.

Ramos, Julio. *Desencuentros de la modernidad en América Latina. Literatura y política en el siglo XIX*. Mexico: FCE, 1989.

Rancière, Jacques. *On the Shores of Politics*. Translated by Liz Heron. London: Verso, 1995.

———. *Dis-agreement: Politics and Philosophy*. Translated by Julie Rose. Minneapolis: University of Minnesota Press, 1999.

Rest, Jaime. *El cuarto en el recoveco*. Buenos Aires: CEAL, 1982.

———. *Literatura y cultura de masas*. Buenos Aires: CEAL, 1967.

Ritvo, Juan B. *La edad de la lectura*. Rosario: Beatriz Viterbo Editora, 1992.

Romano, Eduardo, Abel Posada, et al., *La cultura popular del peronismo*. Buenos Aires: Editorial Cimarrón, 1974.

Romero, José Luis. *Latinoamérica: las ciudades y las ideas*. Mexico: Siglo XXI, 1976.

Ropars-Wuilleumier, Marie-Claire. *L'idée d'image*. Vincennes: PUV, 1995.

Rowe, John Carlos, ed. *Post-Nationalist American Studies*. Berkeley: University of California Press, 2000.

Saer, Juan José. *El concepto de ficción*. Madrid: Alianza, 1991.

———. *El río sin orillas*. Buenos Aires: Ariel, 1997.

Said, Edward. *Culture and Imperialism*. New York: Alfred A. Knopf, 1993.

Sarduy, Severo. *Ensayos generales sobre el barroco*. Mexico: Siglo XXI, 1987.

———. "Barroco y neobarroco." In *América Latina en su literatura*, edited by C. Fernández Moreno. Mexico: Siglo XXI, 1972.

Sarlo, Beatriz. *Una modernidad periférica. Buenos Aires, 1920 y 1930*. Buenos Aires: Nueva Visión, 1988.

Sarmiento, D. F. *Facundo o civilización y barbarie en las pampas argentinas*. Buenos Aires: CEAL, 1979.

Scholem, Gershom. *Kabbalah*. New York: Penguin, 1978.

Smith, Anna Marie. *Laclau and Mouffe: the Radical Democratic Imaginary*. London: Routledge, 1998.

Stabb, Martin S. *In Quest of Identity: Patterns in the Spanish American Essay of Ideas, 1890–1960*. Chapel Hill: University of North Carolina Press, 1967.

Subirats, Eduardo. *Figuras de la conciencia desdichada*. Madrid: Taurus, 1979.

Van Den Abbeele, Georges. *Travel as Metaphor: From Montaigne to Rousseau*. Minneapolis: University of Minnesota Press, 1992.

Vitier, Medardo. *Del ensayismo americano*. Mexico: FCE, 1945.

Warminski, Andrej. *Readings in Interpretation: Hölderlin, Hegel, Heidegger*. Minneapolis: University of Minnesota Press, 1987.

Weber, Samuel. *Mass Mediarus: Form, Technics, Media*. Stanford: Stanford University Press, 1996.

Yúdice, George, J. Flores, and J. Franco, eds. *On Edge: The Crisis of Contemporary Latin American Culture*. Minneapolis: Universiy of Minnesota Press, 1992.

Zerilli, Linda M. G. "The Universalism Which is Not One." *Diacritics* 28, no. 2 (1998).

Ziarek, Ewa. "'The Beauty of Failure': Kafka and Benjamin on the Task of Transmission and Translation." In *Unruly Examples: On the Rhetoric of Exemplarity*, edited by A. Gelley. Stanford: Stanford University Press, 1995.

Žižek, Slavoj. *For They Know Not What They Do: Enjoyment as a Political Factor*. London: Verso, 1991.

———. *The Ticklish Subject*. London: Verso, 1999.

Index

150